Daddy,

I know we will be moving soon & I want you to 'member where I was born.

I love you, Daddy!

Liam
xmas '98

# James Herriot's Yorkshire

# James Herriot's Yorkshire

## with photographs by Derry Brabbs

LONDON

MICHAEL JOSEPH

*To*
*my grandchildren*
*Emma and Nicholas*
*in the hope that they*
*will discover Yorkshire for themselves*

# Contents

MICHAEL JOSEPH LTD
Published by the Penguin Group
27 Wrights Lane, London W8 5TZ, England
Viking Penguin Inc., 375 Hudson Street, New York, New York 10014, USA
Penguin Books Australia Ltd, Ringwood, Victoria, Australia
Penguin Books Canada Ltd, 10 Alcorn Avenue, Toronto, Ontario, Canada M4V 3B2
Penguin Books (NZ) Ltd, 182–190 Wairau Road, Auckland 10, New Zealand

Penguin Books Ltd, Registered Offices: Harmondsworth, Middlesex, England

© 1979 James Herriot Partnership
© Photographs 1979 by Michael Joseph Ltd

1st impression October 1979, 22nd impression December 1996

ISBN 0 7181 1735 0 Casebound ISBN 07181 2144 9 Paperback
Printed and bound by Bookprint, Barcelona, Spain.

# My Yorkshire

I suppose you could say my Yorkshire is contained between two lines drawn from the heads of Coverdale and Swaledale, across the plain of York and over the Hambleton Hills and the North York Moors to the enchanting villages and towns of the east coast.

On a map they would not appear as straight lines. The top one, stretching from just above Keld to Marske-by-the-Sea, would have many wobbles, and the bottom one, from the wild country at the head of the river Cover would also undulate considerably on its way to Scarborough with two enormous bulges to take in Harrogate and York.

Some of the country between these lines I know only slightly, other parts are reasonably familiar while there are many places where every pebble is like an old friend. In any case it is between these lines that I have worked as a veterinary surgeon, brought up my family, played and holidayed for nearly forty years. I know that there are other glories in this, the biggest county in England. There are several entirely different Yorkshires, but this is mine.

When I left Glasgow to work as assistant to Siegfried Farnon I had the conviction, like many Scots, that there was no scenery outside Scotland. I had a mental impression of Yorkshire as a stodgy, uninteresting place – rural in parts, perhaps, but dull.

I remember Siegfried saying to me, a few days after I had first met him, "Wait till you see Swaledale, Wensleydale and Coverdale, my boy." We had a partner, Frank Bingham, in Leyburn and in those early days I spent much of my time in the Pennines. Siegfried was right. I suddenly found myself in a wonderland.

I think the exact moment when it dawned on me that Yorkshire was a magical place was when I pulled my car off the unfenced road which leads from Leyburn over Bellerby Moor to Grinton. It was around the highest point, by a little stream, and I looked back over the swelling moorland to the great wooded

*My first view of the valley of the Swale*

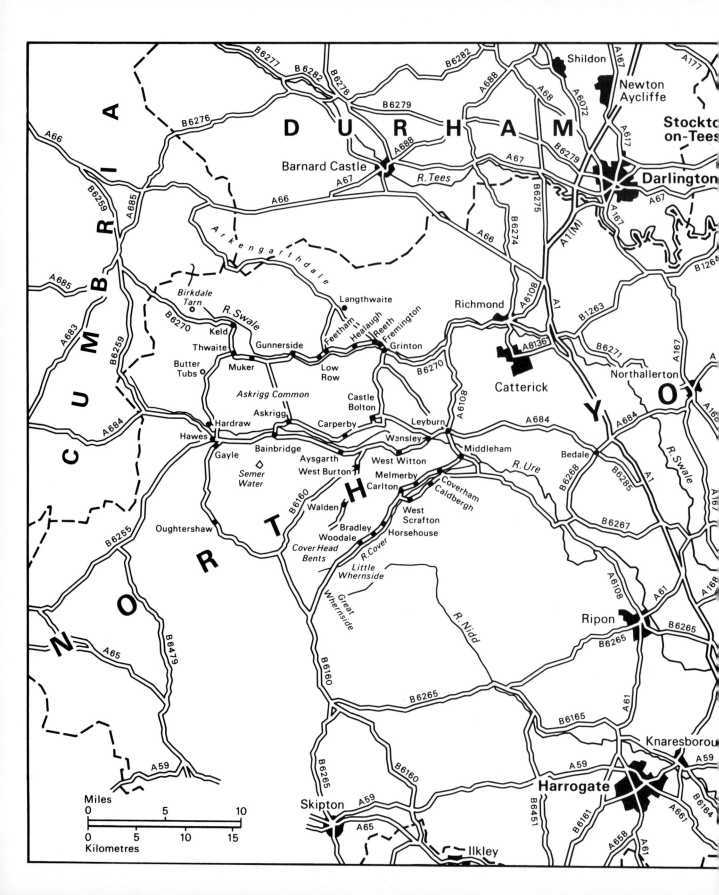

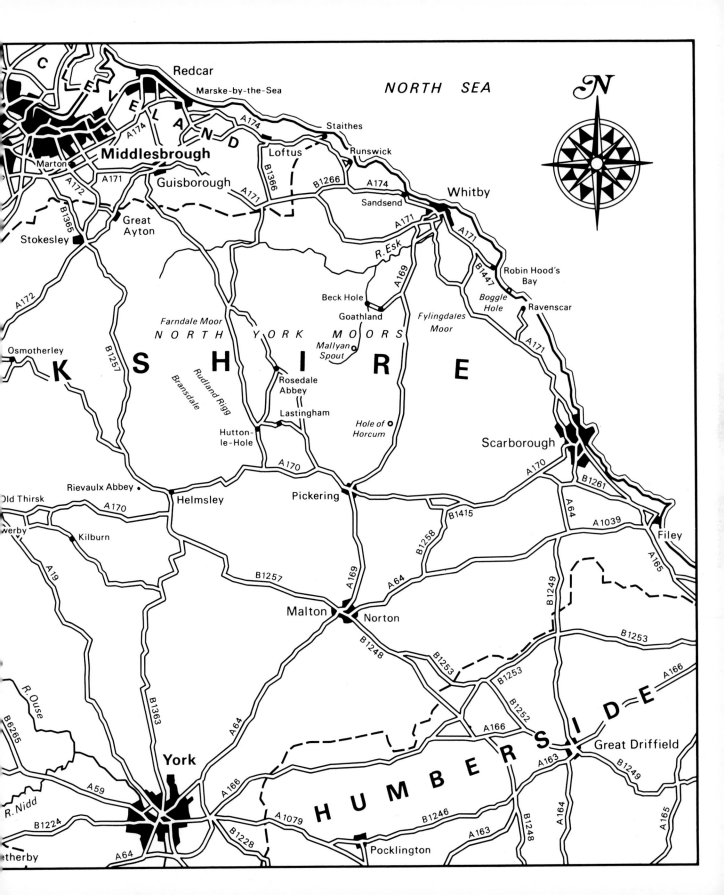

valley of the Swale where it curves on its approach to Richmond.

I gazed at the scene in disbelief. There was everything here; wildness and solitude breathing from the bare fells, yet a hint of softness where the river wound along the valley floor. And in all the green miles around me there was not another human being to be seen.

I got out of the car and sat on the springy grass as I have done on countless occasions since then. I was captivated, completely spellbound and I still am to this day.

I was in my early twenties then and this was only the first inkling of the glories my veterinary work was to unfold for me. It was to take me into the wildest country at the head of the three Dales, to Bradley and Woodale, Gayle and Keld, villages bordered by the bleakest country in England. Vets were thin on the ground in those days and Frank Bingham's practice extended into the remotest corners.

This high country is just too bleak for some people but it is up there on the empty moors with the curlews crying that I have been able to find peace and tranquillity of mind.

*The river Swale outside Keld and (above) through Richmond.*

It is a land of pure air, rocky streams and hidden waterfalls. In the winter the roads are often impassable when the heavy snow falls and the high fells are a white wilderness where a man could easily lose his way and die. But on summer days when the sun beats down on the lonely miles these uplands are a paradise, the air heavy with the sweetness of warm grass, the breeze carrying a thousand scents from the valley below.

I like my fellow men but there are times when it is wonderful to be utterly alone in a wide landscape. There aren't many places in England where you can do this, but you can do it in my Yorkshire.

*Scenes in a Yorkshire winter*

My veterinary work also took me all over the Hambleton Hills and on to the edge of the North York Moors. This whetted my appetite to explore this region and I found a spacious, airy country of heather and deep gills. Ryedale, Bransdale, and Farndale with its incredible carpet of daffodils in the spring. These moors sweep for nearly fifty miles from the Hambletons to the North Sea. Near the coast in August, when the heather is in full bloom, the rich heady scent mingled with the salty tang of the sea, is something which I have not found anywhere else in England.

Beyond the North York Moors the heather-clad country dips into a strip of coast of rare charm. The quaint fishing villages are themselves rich in character, but the miles of sea-washed sand have made them an irresistible attraction for holidaymakers.

When I first came to Yorkshire I was too busy to see much of the east coast but my six months in Scarborough in the RAF, which I describe in my books, gave me an insight into the unique beauty of the area. I resolved that I would come back after the war and seek out all the places I was unable to see as I marched and drilled in RAF blue.

As I have said, the first thing that enthralled me about Yorkshire was its wild beauty, the feeling of remoteness and solitude which keeps one's sense of wonder alive, but as time went on I realised there was something else – the strong ambience of history. The distant past seemed somehow close at hand.

Everywhere there are the reminders, the inspiring evidence of bygone things. The abbey ruins of Rievaulx, Fountains, Byland, Whitby; the smaller, poignant remnants of Marrick Priory, the Knights' Templar Chapel near Swinithwaite; the fine old castles of Bolton, Middleham, Richmond, Helmsley. There are many more, and what fun we had with our children exploring these places. Then of course there are the tremendous cathedrals of York and Ripon, preserved intact for fortunate posterity to view.

Out on the high tops there are many tumuli, barrows and ancient forts to recall the presence of prehistoric man. There are Roman remains, as in the Roman camp at Bainbridge and the many straight roads. The A66 highway from Scotch Corner was the original Watling Street and the locals still refer to it as "The Street".

*The ruins of Whitby Abbey (left) and Marrick Priory.*

Most fascinating of all, perhaps, is the everyday reminders of the occupation of the Norsemen, in the names of the villages – Caldbergh in Coverdale and the innumerable hamlets ending in "by". A Swedish journalist who accompanied me on my rounds for a day was deeply intrigued by the similarity of the place names in our practice to those in Scandinavia.

The strange intermixture of past and present was brought home to me one day while doing a tuberculin test on a farm in Coverdale. When moving from one cowhouse to another, I came suddenly upon the stone effigies of two knights in chain armour. I was startled to be confronted by these weathered relics of the thirteenth century and baffled, too, till it was explained to me that the farm was built on the site of Coverham Abbey of which little now remains. The two figures were of Ranulph FitzRobert, the founder of the abbey, and his son, Ralph FitzRanulph.

When I think back over the years in my part of Yorkshire, it is my beginnings which are most vivid. My first meeting with Siegfried, my early days with Frank Bingham. Siegfried, happily, is still my partner and friend but Frank died many years ago, like many good vets, in a cow byre doing a tough job.

He was much older than Siegfried or myself, fifty-eight when I first met him, but youthful-looking and handsome. I have never met a man I liked better and I based the character Ewan Ross in my books on Frank, not just because he was a fine person, but because he was somebody way out of the ordinary. He and his charming and talented wife, Emmy, treated me with the greatest kindness.

Frank had spent most of his life wandering the world, usually doing something connected with horses. He had been in the Canadian North West Mounted Police, he had spent years riding the Australian rabbit fences, in fact he had lived in the saddle most of his days and could roll a cigarette with one hand as the cowboys do in the films.

*The sun breaks through storm clouds over Coverdale*

He came to Britain with the Australian expeditionary force at the outbreak of the first world war and qualified as a veterinary surgeon soon after.

I suppose it wasn't surprising that Frank was a heaven-sent expert with horses. He knew the practical as well as the theoretical side of the business, which a lot of us don't. For a green young vet like me, to see him in action was an education in itself and he was the only man I have ever seen rope and throw a wild young colt single-handed.

The Binghams made Leyburn something special for me and it has always remained so. My strongest memories were their personal kindness to me. Frank's soft-spoken humorous welcome every time I went up to Leyburn, Emmy's friendly teasing and her wonderful cooking.

The present-day vets at Leyburn are my friends but even now, when I pass through the town, I feel a dull ache when I see the Binghams' little house at the foot of the hill and realise they are no longer there.

And at this moment, when I look down on the map at this dearly familiar segment of my own piece of

*Foals. (Left) Bransdale seen from the top of Cowhouse Bank*

Yorkshire, I can see and recall all the places so clearly; where I have calved cows, foaled mares, found heady success and abject failure, laughed or had my heart nearly broken.

I have put a lot of it in my books but of course the names of places and people are all changed because when I first started to write at the advanced age of fifty, I thought it would stop at one book and nobody would ever discover the identity of the obscure veterinary surgeon who had scribbled his experiences in snatched moments of spare time.

This has caused a lot of nice people all over the world much puzzlement as they searched their travel books in vain. Where for instance is Darrowby? I really don't know myself. It is a composite town; a bit of Thirsk, something of Richmond, Leyburn and Middleham and a fair chunk of my own imagination.

Between the two lines on my map I can recall the great multitude of Shorthorn cattle which grazed those fields. In the early days you never saw anything but a Shorthorn in these parts and it was incredible that within a few years the lovely roans and reds would be engulfed and swept away by the flood of black and white Friesians.

And now those black and white beasts are being diluted by the ever-increasing duns and golds of the Charollais and other imported breeds.

Those magnificent Shires and Clydesdale horses are gone, too, from the farms. The tractor is king except in a few isolated instances.

So many things have changed, even the farmers. I think they have altered most of all; the hard-bitten old characters with their idiosyncrasies and their black magic cures who formed such a fertile source for my writing are very hard to find now. They have been largely replaced by the new breed of highly knowledgeable young men whose skill has made British agriculture the most efficient in the world,

*View from the Hawes to Askrigg road*

but who are not as interesting as their forefathers.

But, thank heaven, the Dales haven't changed. The dry stone walls still climb up the bare hillsides as they have always done. Those wonderful walls, often the only sign of the hand of man, symbolise the very soul of the high Pennines, the endlessly varying pattern of grey against green, carving out ragged squares and oblongs, pushing long antennae to impossible heights till they disappear into the lapping moorland on the summits.

It is a constant marvel to me that, long ago, men just slapped flat stones one on top of the other on those dizzy gradients and left them to stand there in all weathers for hundreds of years. It wasn't as easy as that, of course; it was a highly skilled and intricate job which has become to a great extent a lost art.

But what I see most clearly on my map is the little stretch of velvet grass by the river's edge where I camped or picnicked with my family. I can see the golden beach where my children built their castles in the sand. These are the parts, when my children were young, which stand out most vividly from the coloured paper.

These indeed, as I look down on my Yorkshire, are the sweet places of memory.

*Some of Yorkshire's fascinating wall patterns*

# Bedale

This is the typical little Yorkshire market town through which I passed a thousand times on my way from Siegfried's practice to Frank Bingham's.

I always looked on it as the gateway to the Dales. A long street, cobbled on either side, with a slim market cross and the big tower of St Gregory's church facing me.

After Bedale the ground begins to rise imperceptibly and very soon the first outlines of the Pennines begin to appear and you can see the big fells at the entrance to Coverdale and Wensleydale looming and beckoning.

One snag about that rising ground is that it gets more snow and in the heavy falls of forty years ago it was usually just beyond Bedale that I came upon blocked roads and had to turn back.

*The busy market town Bedale: the way to Leyburn and the Dales*

# Youth Hostels

It just happens that some of my favourite country in the North Yorkshire Pennines is enclosed in a triangle formed by three Youth Hostels – Aysgarth, Grinton and Keld, and it would be as good a way as any of showing you the district to describe one of my walks round these hostels.

As a boy in Glasgow I had been an inveterate camper, escaping from the veterinary college every weekend to sleep under canvas at Rosneath on The Gareloch or by a stream high on the Campsie Hills above Fintry. I have to admit that when my son Jimmy asked me to go youth hostelling with him for a long weekend, I was inclined to look down my nose at the whole idea.

It seemed a little effete to spend the night under a solid roof, but I allowed myself to be persuaded and we set off from Leyburn one Friday afternoon in August along with Ian Brown, one of Jimmy's school friends.

Leyburn has a thousand happy associations for me. Architecturally, it is not a glamorous place but its situation is exciting. If Bedale is the gateway to the Dales, then Leyburn is right on the doorstep. You can slip over Bellerby Moor into Swaledale, turn off through Middleham into Coverdale or go straight ahead down Wensleydale. My three dales are all at hand.

Old books talk about Leyburn's reputation for longevity in its inhabitants and indeed one can imagine its being a healthy town, perched up on that breezy hillside with the main road climbing to the wide market place at the top. When I first visited Leyburn to work for Frank Bingham I was shown with pride The Shawl, a two-miles long terrace walk above the escarpment to the west of the town. The outlook from there is very fine and its unusual name comes from the Scandinavian *schall* – a collection of huts. Probably this was the site of the original settlement.

*Leyburn : the crowded market place and the lovely view from the Shawl*

With the two boys I headed for the top left-hand corner of the market place. Aysgarth was our first objective and we set off down the hill towards Wensley.

I felt the same thrill I have always felt at that spot. The road dips, and quite suddenly the town is left behind and the whole wide gracious vista of Wensleydale opens up beneath you. My heart lifted as the majestic bulk of Penhill loomed before us, the lower slopes sprinkled with trees and the flat summit with its bare moorland thrusting into the clouds.

Our rucksacks were settling comfortably on our shoulders as we swung into the quiet village of Wensley. The big gates at the entrance to Bolton Hall add to its air of gentleness and grace and, looking across to the thirteenth-century church on our left, my thoughts turned to the tragedy of Wensley. It was once an important market town, regarded, in fact, as the capital of the Dale, but in 1563 it was ravaged by a deadly plague. Many of its habitants perished and most of the others fled in terror from the pestilence.

It seemed a desecration that such horror and sadness should ever have existed in this tranquil setting of grey stones and river and green hillsides, but it happened and Wensley never recovered. It shrank within itself, its bustling market disappeared and was taken over by Leyburn and the place became the sleepy village it has been for the last four hundred years.

*Wensley village and its church where I was married in the TV series* All Creatures Great and Small

A smaller road goes off to the right to Redmire and Carperby but we kept to the south route and crossed the big stone bridge over the Ure. The sun blazed, our boots clattered on the tarmac and we looked around us at a landscape from which the fences had disappeared. Everywhere there were the dry stone walls enclosing the pastures with their carpet of wild flowers and all the time Penhill on the left, calm and massive, dominated the scene.

I saw the road to Spigot Lodge curving up the flanks of the great fell. Colonel Lyde had his racing stables there in those days and I gazed upwards towards the high fields where Siegfried and I had carried out so many horse operations. Open stretches of grass are the country vet's operating table and there was none better than those up there where my intravenous Pentothal had sent so many sleek thoroughbreds thudding to the ground.

Soon we were entering West Witton, once a mining village – a long straggle of houses nestling beneath the hill and the road to the left climbing over to Melmerby in Coverdale. That road with its hairpin bends is carved permanently in my memory. It may be nothing special to the ordinary motorist but it is horrific to the driver of a car with no brakes.

Towards the end of the village on the right is a nice little pub, the Wensleydale Heifer, where Helen and I have had many meals over the years. Probably the most memorable was our second wedding anniversary dinner with Frank and Emmy Bingham when we also stayed overnight.

Beyond West Witton we could see the entire breadth of the beautiful Dale with Bolton Castle, grim and square, jutting from the green slopes on the

*Dry stone walls. (Opposite, top) the attractive Wensleydale Heifer at West Witton and (bottom) Bolton Castle in winter*

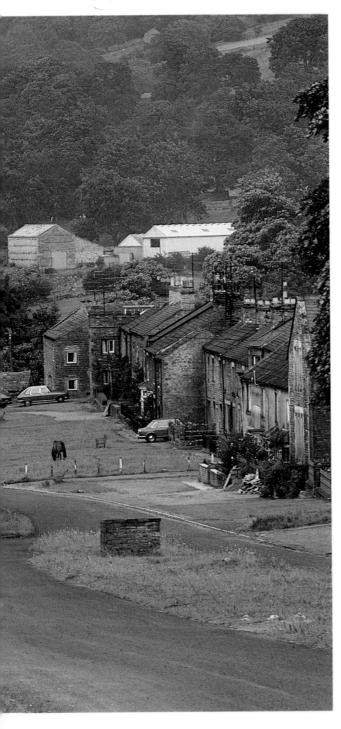

*Beautiful West Burton*

other side. The Scropes built their great fortress in the fourteenth century in the perfect position to command a distant view of the Dale from all sides. Its most romantic association is the fact that it held Mary Queen of Scots as a prisoner for six months in 1568, but to me the appeal of the castle is in its situation – all-seeing and visible from such great distances, dwarfing its surroundings.

At that moment as we marched along it was wonderful how many familiar farms I could see and the memories from each place jostled in my mind.

That one over there, for instance. When we were first married and Helen used to come with me a lot on my rounds, I stitched up a cow's teat in that ancient byre. The farmer was an old man and when he saw me back to my car, he peered in long and earnestly at Helen in the passenger seat.

He crooked a finger at me and as I bent towards him he whispered in my ear.

"You've done t'right thing, lad. If I had me time over again, that's what I'd 'ave done."

I was a little mystified. "What do you mean?"

"Well ah'll tell ye." He glanced furtively towards the door of the farmhouse. "Ah'd have got summat to look at."

I couldn't remember what his wife looked like, but it did seem a little unkind at the time.

For a while the huge roadside trees formed a canopy of leaves above us, shutting out the sky, then we were striding past Temple Farm, so called because the ruins of the Knights' Templar Chapel stand on the hillside opposite.

It wasn't long before we saw the entrance of the road leading to West Burton, acclaimed by some as the most beautiful village in England. This is saying a lot, but it is without doubt a lovely place – a classical Yorkshire village with its long central green. We weren't going down there this time, in any case, but as we left the road behind us my mind was wandering

away through the village and into the seductive little valley of Walden behind it.

I am particularly in love with the narrow track on the east side of Walden and it is one of Helen's favourite places. To drive up there, high above the tree-lined Walden Beck, is to escape easily from the workaday world. And if you leave your car and walk the old path over the moor till the fell tilts into Coverdale and the vast stream-furrowed face of Little Whernside rears up across the valley, you will be richly rewarded.

But we were fast approaching Aysgarth, the ground began to rise quite sharply and as we puffed our way upwards we saw on the corner the massive stone building of the Youth Hostel.

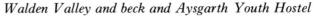

*Walden Valley and beck and Aysgarth Youth Hostel*

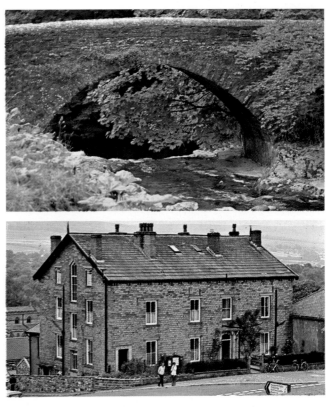

Following the instructions of the boys, I removed my heavy boots and pulled on a pair of plimsolls before entering. This, it seemed, was the rule. We dumped our rucksacks by our beds and set off for the dining-room. I had feared that at the age of forty I might be regarded as rather an old-fashioned youth, but I was relieved to find many grey heads around me. In fact there were people of all ages including families with quite young children, and we had two things in common – we had all reached here by our own physical effort and we were all hungry.

I soon realised that we had come to the right place for hungry people. The bare boards and spartan furnishings of the hostel had not prepared me for the

*Aysgarth church and the ancient gravestones*

sumptuous meal of soup, steak pie with two veg and apple pie and custard. I had barely recovered from this by breakfast time when porridge was served by the gallon. I noticed lean young fellows marching up again and again to refill their plates and dowse them with milk from the tall jugs on the long tables. Bacon, eggs, sausage and fried bread followed, then everybody started hacking at the rows of loaves and plastering the slices with marmalade. When the last pint of tea had gone down, the walkers were ready to face the road.

The prices were interesting. The accommodation cost one and sixpence each, dinner was two and six, breakfast two shillings, and if you were one of the hardy "self-cookers", the use of the kitchen was available for three of the old pennies.

Of course, everybody had their "chores" to do – I swept out the dormitory while the boys helped with the dish-washing – but that was a trifling matter.

Before we set off we had to take a look at the famous Aysgarth Falls which lie just below the hostel. I had seen them countless times before but they still drew me irresistibly down the hill with the church on the right, founded in the twelfth century, and the ancient gravestones leaning askew around it. On the corner of the hill a stone parapet curves above the river and I gazed at it, as I always do, with affection. Many years before, my brakeless car decided to stall on that hill and ran backwards at an alarming speed till it crashed into the parapet. That little wall is only about eighteen inches high but it probably saved my life.

We passed the old Yore Mill, now a carriage museum, on our right and then went over the old pack horse bridge which crosses the river.

We stopped on the bridge and had our first sight of the falls, with the same old feeling of delight. The Ure is a gentle river, making its way quietly along the valley floor till it reaches Aysgarth when it suddenly goes wild, rushes into a rocky gorge and drops two hundred feet in a series of magnificent falls.

The ones on the left are the upper falls. There are middle and lower falls further down and many experts regard them as the most spectacular but these upper falls are the ones I like best; where I have taken my children since babyhood and where I have returned with fresh enchantment so many times over the years. Today, as we leaned on the stones of the bridge, the peaty water roared over great rocky slabs and shelves of awe-inspiring size. The river here has infinitely varying moods – it can be a torrent after much rain or snow but in very dry weather there might be only a trickle with children playing on the flat rocks in mid stream.

We turned at the end of the bridge and climbed a path to the river's edge. It is wonderful here. Behind, a green sward rises gently to a little hill, in front the falls tumble beneath the over-hanging branches and across the river the steep wall of the gorge is gloomy with the trees growing from the crevices in its dark face. We followed a little sandy path by the water's edge. I have always found something exciting about it, creeping its solitary way under the trees with the dark river lapping it and that tremendous tree-covered wall of rock on the other side.

*The upper falls in summer and a riverside tree*

It is a secret place, a place of wonder, and even on summer Sundays when trippers abound on the stretch of grass, it still preserves its magic. Today, there were only the three of us making our way over the naked roots of the trees and there was no sound but the eternal bubbling of the river between its stones and the muted roar of the falls behind us. Among the dark verdure on the other side of the river, the smell of wild garlic was strong. Right at the end of the path, the Ure reverts to its normal character, a quiet-flowing, placid stream.

But we had to be on our way. Back to the hostel and off through Aysgarth village to where the road drops and Wensleydale again lays out her full charms, now with the fells on the far side the highest. The rocky outcrops on their summits command the scene as Penhill did before.

But a feeling of unease had begun to nag at me. Dark clouds were driving up from the west and there was a chill dampness in the air.

"Get moving lads," I said. "It could rain today and we've got fifteen miles to go. If the rain does come, I just hope it doesn't start on the moor."

I was a bit worried. To reach Keld, in Swaledale, we had to cross a barren stretch of wasteland on the huge ridge between the two valleys, covering Askrigg Common and Oxnop, and there wasn't a stick of shelter anywhere along the way. I didn't like getting wet – I preferred to dive into a barn at the slightest shower – and I kept muttering to myself, "Oh, I hope it doesn't rain on the moor. Oh, don't let it rain over Oxnop," to the great amusement of Ian and Jimmy who weren't bothered by such things.

We made our way through Worton and crossed the river, gentle and pebbly here, to the other side of the Dale, and a brisk walk brought us to the outskirts of Askrigg. We had to turn sharp right on the road to Swaledale so we did not see much of the dignified old village in its beautiful setting. It has a cobbled market place and market cross and a thirteenth-century church and in the picture shown is the house which was used as Skeldale House in the TV series.

We were now on a really steep hill with a gradient of one in four. It was hard going, up and up, twisting at first between the houses, then between occasional barns and the eternal walls. It was good to stop now and again to take a breath and to be able to see all of Askrigg laid out against the great back-cloth of Wensleydale.

*Askrigg and its version of Skeldale House*

But my enjoyment of the scene was marred by the leaden sky which pressed down, dark and lowering, as we climbed. "Oh, please don't let it rain on the top," I moaned again. "Don't let it rain over Oxnop." And the boys giggled.

Gradually, as our surroundings grew wilder, we left the last of the barns behind and there before us was the gate to the moor. That gate was just about the last touch of civilisation for more than five miles. Here the graciousness and softness of Wensleydale was far away and an empty vastness stretched to the horizon on every side. Not a house, not a building, not a sign of man.

I opened the gate and we passed through. And there is no doubt that the weather man in the sky has a sense of humour. It seemed as though he was determined to get his timing perfect. "Hold it there, chaps, just a second more," he was saying to his minions. Then at the very instant I dropped the latch and turned towards the yawning moorland, he roared, "Okay, let it go!"

From the dark canopy above, a solid sheet of water fell upon us. It never stopped all through the rest of that day.

We struggled into our capes, pulling them over our rucksacks, which made us look like three streaming hunchbacks, and headed forward. After two or three miles we had reached the top of the high plateau but still, as I glanced up from my head-down plodding, I could see no sign of human habitation, only the sodden heather, the sparse grass and the peat hags.

We passed a sign saying "To Muker" and we had our first view of the soaring mounds on the far side of Swaledale. One of the exquisite pleasures of the north Pennines is passing from dale to dale, the looking back and the eager anticipation of the unfolding beauty to come. That was how it should have been that day, but it was difficult to appreciate anything with the rain flooding down my neck and trickling in steady rivulets down my cape on to my calf muscles.

The tittering from the rear didn't help either. The boys, striding behind me, appeared to find something irresistibly funny about my fearful foreboding and this dramatic denouement. The constant drip-drip on to my bare legs (shorts were *de rigueur* for hikers in those days) completed their enjoyment. In fact, all these years later, they still chuckle happily about it.

But as I say, I didn't feel at all cheerful. From the corner of my eye, I saw that we were passing huge outcrops of rock and scree-lined slopes which made the scene even more desolate.

Then at last, perhaps a mile ahead, a barn appeared. But it was too late now – we were thoroughly soaked. We squelched our way through another white gate on to a narrow road which dipped sharply and tortuously between its walls and at one of the last bends we had a sudden view of much of the length of Swaledale – a heavenly vision of peace on sunny days, and even in this driving rain a sight to lift the heart. The towering green slopes, smooth and unbroken except for a single deep gill and the scattering of farmhouses looking down on the pebbly river making its leisurely way along the bed of the valley.

*Wild Oxnop (below) and our sudden view of Swaledale*

A final steep bend and we were on to the Reeth-Muker road. A mile's trudge with the rain bouncing off the tarmac brought us into Muker, one of Swaledale's little dream places with a picturesque stone bridge at the entrance and another just beyond the far end. The building of a church there in 1580 made it no longer necessary to carry the dead from the head of the Dale to the only consecrated ground at Grinton.

The road hugs the beck beyond Muker and after passing a little waterfall, we found ourselves looking down on the tiled roofs of Thwaite. This is a typical Dales village if ever you saw one; the inevitable hump-backed bridge, the massive houses of grey stone, the whole clustered atmosphere suggesting a nearness to the head of the Dale. But at that moment, all our attention was centred on one thing. A shop. A shop with an open door.

It was only three o'clock in the afternoon and the hostel at Keld would not open till five. We were away ahead of our time because we had been striding doggedly non-stop all day instead of lazing on the moor top as we had planned. We had to find some shelter, and the warm interior of the shop beckoned us urgently.

*Muker under snow and (opposite, bottom and below) two views of Thwaite*

"Could I have three bars of chocolate, please?" I said to the man behind the counter.

He smiled, apparently undismayed by the three dripping creatures before him.

"Certainly, by all means." He handed over three bars of Rowntree's Fruit and Nut and we began to nibble at them with infinite deliberation.

"Wonderful selection you have here." I bit off another quarter inch and began to chew unhurriedly.

"Yes," replied the shopkeeper. "We try to keep a bit of all sorts." He looked round his shelves proudly. He was a charming man and fortunately seemed to enjoy conversation. He enlarged upon how he kept the village and surrounding farms supplied, and discussed the relative merits of pilchards and sardines, of boiled ham and tongue. Every word was like a pearl.

He had got round most of his stock and our chocolate was finished when I glanced through the door at the rain still churning the puddles in the village street.

"I think we could do with some of those salted peanuts," I said.

As I opened my bag I tried another tack. "I expect you get a fair number of visitors up here in the summer?"

"We certainly do." His eyes brightened and he raised a finger as he described some of the townspeople who ventured into the high Pennines. We munched happily and listened.

It turned out that he ran a guest house in the village quite near his shop and again with pride he gave us mouth-watering details of meals his wife provided for the holiday-makers. I love talking about food, especially when I have a sound roof over my head and the rain is pounding down a few feet away, and I drew the hospitable chap out on the subject. But at last even this splendid topic began to wear a little thin so I ordered an orange apiece.

It took us a long time to peel these and I felt guilty when I saw the pools around our feet from the water

which had run off us, but the smile on the good man's face never altered. Clearly, he didn't mind in the least.

When the last orange segment had been consumed, I looked at my watch. We would just about reach Keld in time. As we headed along the road he waved us off from his doorway. Bending against the rain, I thanked providence that Dales shopkeepers were just as hospitable as the farmers.

We were in the wild country now and though we had only about two miles to go, it seemed a long long way as the road curved and turned between its walls and the bare fells rose into the wet sky with remote, isolated farms clinging to their flanks.

Keld lies beneath the road and we didn't enter it but made straight for the tall hostel standing high on our left. The warden was just opening the door as we reached it. He was a well-built man with a heavy

*The hostel at Keld and (left) the Thwaite side of Kisdon Hill*

black moustache and the corner of his mouth twitched into a half smile as he surveyed the three drenched mortals on the step.

"Leave your boots here," he said. It seemed he was a man who didn't waste words.

We went upstairs, pulled dry clothes from our rucksacks and changed. We towelled our heads, had a good hot water wash and came down feeling much better. The first things we saw were our three pairs of boots, stuffed with newspapers, dangling in a row round an old iron stove. They would be dry when we started out again, a bonus thrown in for our one and sixpence accommodation charge.

Keld was quite a small hostel and there were only six other occupants of the little dining-room looking out over the road. The warden served us with delicious fish and chips for our evening meal and a massive breakfast in the morning. When asking us to do our chores, he murmured, "Perhaps you and your young men would give me a hand with a few little jobs." Soft-voiced, slow-smiling, he was, like our shopkeeper, a nice man and I look back on both of them with affection.

Hoisting our rucksacks on our backs we stepped out into a different world. The sun shone, a few white clouds drifted over a canopy of blue, and how can I describe the first breath of scented air? I love Spain with its sunshine but much of it is arid and you can't smell the countryside. Whenever I come back from a holiday there, the first thing I notice is the Dales smell – and this morning, after all the rain, it was multiplied. A great wave drifting over the miles of grass, carrying the fragrance of moorland turf, wild flowers and every growing thing. It lapped around us as we walked down into the village.

Keld is from the Scandinavian *kelda*, a spring or stream, and looking at the huddle of grey houses tucked in and hidden among the fells it was easy to see why the old Vikings made their settlement there. It is a perfect sheltered retreat and a refuge from enemies.

Apart from its beauty, there is a thrill of being in Keld because you know you are at the head of Swaledale. This is the last and highest village. Its surroundings are dominated by the peaceful bulk of Kisdon Hill, often called Kisdon Island in old books and maps because it is cut off by water on all sides — by the Swale on the north and east, by Skeb Skeugh Beck on the west and Muker Beck on the south.

Hundreds of years ago, funeral processions made their way over Kisdon along a track known as the Corpse Way which led to the nearest consecrated ground at Grinton, twelve miles away. The dead were carried here from the head of the dale and there are stone slabs along the route where the coffins were rested.

There are fine falls near Keld, the Catrake and Kisdon Falls, but we had visited them before and decided to take the hill path to Gunnerside. At the foot of the village we turned right down a narrow stony path with crumbling walls on either side, through a gate at the foot, and there was the wooden bridge over the river. Here the Swale has cut its way through a deep ravine and winds under trees and over shelving rocks.

*The Swale near Wain Wath Force. (Below) near Keld*

Fascinated, we lingered on the bridge, watching the tumbling of the dark water in its gorge – a real piece of Yorkshire, this. But at length we had to leave and took the path upwards over another little bridge and headed for Swinnergill.

We came upon Crackpot Hall, a romantic house built as a shooting lodge for Lord Wharton to hunt the deer which roamed this part of Swaledale early in the eighteenth century. When the deer disappeared it became a farm, but when Jimmy, Ian and I stood before it that day it was deserted and the roof looked ready to fall in. In fact the windows and walls leaned at crazy angles due possibly to subsidence from the mines beneath. At the moment of writing, the place is a ruin but it still has the sad splendour which the boys and I found on that day twenty years ago.

The tumbled stones look out on a matchless landscape of moor and fell and I could not but envy the people who once dwelt there.

We tramped through Swinnergill and over Melbecks Moor to Gunnerside Gill. We didn't hurry over this part of the journey but lay down often on the springy turf, heads on our rucksacks, and took the sun on our faces as we gazed around us at the wonder of those grassy uplands. I felt again that nowhere is the Dales ambience of peace and mountain air so strong as in that country above Crackpot Hall.

It seemed to me that I could never be unhappy here, or plagued by the little worries of the world. "Away from it all" is an over-worked phrase but anybody who wants to know what it really means should try this walk. I once stood on the top of the Jungfrau (I hadn't climbed it but was carried there in a train along with 800 other people). Standing up there in the crush among the snow, I felt nothing – it didn't mean a thing. No, I felt nothing on the Jungfrau but I felt a million miles from reality above Crackpot.

We carried on across Gunnerside Gill to see the massive, haunting remains of the Old Gang Mines

*The view from Crackpot Hall*

and the smelt mills lower down. After seeing no evidence of man for hours, it is always a shock to come upon those forlorn relics of a lost industry cupped in the silent moors.

We then retraced our step into the Gill and made great speed down that most beguiling of grassy tracks into Gunnerside.

Gunnerside! There is a Norse name for you. Gunnar's Pasture, where a Viking chief herded his livestock many centuries ago. Now it is a most appealing village with pretty little houses climbing up the hillside and a glorious view along the valley.

It is difficult to imagine that between the old Nordic days and now it was once one of the great centres of the lead mining industry, closely involved with the Old Gang Mines. The name of the mines suggests their age, "Gang" being Old English for road, and some authorities claim that they were old when the Saxons came here in the sixth and seventh centuries.

Beyond Gunnerside, our road took us close by the river, a curving avenue of constant enchantment, a long delight of unfolding views of green fells, scattered grey barns and always the pebbly river at its heart. The feeling of peace was almost palpable.

We were very hot when we came into Low Row and stopped for a glass of lemonade at the Punch Bowl Inn. This is a justly renowned establishment and many years later we took Jimmy and a friend to dinner there in the course of his arduous conquest of the Pennine Way.

Today, the landlord of the Punch Bowl is a Harley Street doctor who suddenly grew tired of city life and traffic jams, renounced his previous existence and moved to Swaledale. He has never regretted it, and when you look from the inn over the valley at the green hills with their smudges of heather, you can

understand that he has ample recompense for the things he has left behind. Only recently, too, Robert Hardy, the famous actor who took the part of Siegfried in the TV series, made the Punch Bowl his headquarters during the filming.

I might add here that from Feetham, just beyond Low Row, a beautiful little side road turns off to Arkengarthdale. This is the road used by the TV people in the introductory scenes to the weekly episodes. James and Siegfried are seen laughing together in their car as they drive over a bridge, then a ford. The real ford is on this road and the bridge is at Langthwaite in Arkengarthdale.

Next, through Feetham to Healaugh and when we had passed, I looked up the long fellside to Riddings Farm perched so high that you wondered why they put it there. I recalled a spring day when I was tuberculin testing for Frank Bingham and I came out of the cow byre and looked down on a scene far below which has stayed in my memory. The river, widening into shallow loops, the waters glittering and dancing as they played between their banks of white pebbles; on the right, the green valley stretching away towards its head and on the left, Reeth, Grinton and the

*The widening river Swale. (Opposite, top) the roofs of Gunnerside and the view along the valley. (Bottom) Healaugh*

highway to Richmond. Maybe that was why they put Riddings Farm up there.

We clattered our way into Reeth and quite suddenly everything changed. It was as though a voice said, "All right, that part's finished." The enclosed feeling of walking in a valley was gone; the wildness was gone, too, and the whole countryside opened up into the spaciousness of Reeth's village green. Reeth, the biggest village of the Dale, sits wide and comfortable on its hillside plateau and on a Sunday the cars are plentiful.

The boys and I threaded our way through the trippers and visited one of the shops for ice cream. As we licked at our cones, we looked around us at the beauty which the trappings of civilisation could not disguise.

For make no mistake about it, Reeth is beautiful. Its setting on the slopes of Calver Hill is perfection, the ring of houses with fascinating little alleys wandering among them seem to beckon to the stranger – "Come and seek us out."

It was down one of these alleys, many years later, that Helen, our friend Jean Rae and I stumbled upon the filming of the episode of Mr Myatt, the gipsy and his pony with laminitis as described in my book, *It Shouldn't Happen to a Vet*.

I suddenly found myself face to face with my alter ego, Christopher Timothy. It was our first meeting, as it was with Robert Hardy who was there, too, in his role of Siegfried. Hardy had long been one of my favourite actors and I knew he was incapable of doing anything other than play Siegfried brilliantly, but Chris Timothy was an unknown quantity.

When the series was finally shown on the TV screens of Britain, I was utterly captivated by the way Chris had got inside the skin of the young, diffident, city-bred vet – me – trying to make his way among the earthy farmers of the Yorkshire Dales. And so, fortunately, were many millions of others.

Later, of course, I was to meet the bonny, smiling Carol Drinkwater and breezy Peter Davison. They,

too, were little-known actors but they got Helen and Tristan just right.

While on the subject of filming, the grand old house pictured on the corner of Reeth village green was used as Skeldale House in the cinema film *It Shouldn't Happen to a Vet*. In this I was played by John Alderton who is just as much fun in real life as on the screen. Helen was played by Lisa Harrow and Siegfried by Colin Blakely.

But we had to leave Reeth. Down the hill and past the steep little road to Fremington which brought a wry smile to my face as I thought of the winter's afternoon I had spent there, digging my car out of the snow, time after time, hour after hour.

Over the bridge and into Grinton with its imposing church which until 1580 marked the end of the old Corpse Way.

From Grinton you can get back to Leyburn by going so far along the Richmond road, then turning off to Halfpenny House, but the siren song of the high country always draws me over the unfenced moor road. We had to go that way, in any case, to

*(Opposite) the Swale meandering outside Reeth and the village green. (Below) Reeth's Skeldale House*

reach the hostel and it gave me another chance to look at one of the gems of Grinton, the row of ancient houses and cottages which border the steep road from the village.

As we climbed slowly towards the moor, it struck me again that it would be difficult to find a more picturesque line of dwellings anywhere. They stand on the right, at first close by the road, then on the other side of a little beck, straggling ever higher and giving an unforgettable image of age and mellowness and grace.

Once we had left them behind, we were on the open moor again and almost immediately we were confronted by the hostel, a splendid building like a little castle. It was once the shooting lodge of Colonel Charlesworth.

It was more sophisticated than Keld and there were a lot more people there – walkers, cyclists, anybody

*Grinton church and (right) Grinton Hostel. (Below) looking down on Reeth*

who was able to arrive without motorised transport. In the common-room after the evening meal, there was a lot of friendliness and conversation. We were of all types but we were all interested in the same thing, from the little dark cyclist who amazed us with his accounts of the distances he had covered over the lonely roads to the serious-faced, professorish man who puffed at a pipe as he probed us for our views. His love of the wild country was clearly an obsession, and a fanatical light flickered in his eyes as he stabbed at us with his pipe. "You've never tried Teesdale? Oh, you must, you must. Get over Crossfell sometime, I implore you."

We fed well at Grinton and next morning we prepared for the last lap home. But first we walked a hundred yards back down the road, lay among the scented heather and gazed at the scene beneath us.

I always stop at that spot because it is the place from which Reeth should be seen. The cluster of houses in their encircling hills is something which stays in the mind like a pleasant dream.

That morning, the weekend trippers had gone and there was just the sunlit village with the great hump of Calver hovering over it. Trees gave a softness to the lower slopes but above, the high tops were bare and bleak and between you could see everywhere the ranging pattern of the walls which are the heart of the Dales.

I gazed at the two long arms reaching away behind the houses, one to the dale head, the other to Arkengarthdale. The day before, we had come down from Keld but the memories of the smaller valley came fast. More than a thousand years ago it was Arkil's Garth – the farmers still call their fields garths – and now it was most memorable to me because of Great Punchard Gill near its top where you can walk for miles along a soft green path which is one of the finest of the old mine tracks. You can go up there and over the brow of the moor till you look over the awesome desolation of Stainmore to the tiny cars crawling along a thread which is the A66 to Scotland.

And whenever I see that road I think of the incredible journey in the snow with the incomparable Granville Bennett along that very highway. It was on the way back from a veterinary meeting in Appleby and I have described it all in *Vet in Harness*. But that is another story . . .

I didn't want to leave my place by the Grinton hostel. I am a confirmed heather lier. They talk a lot about pocket spring mattresses these days but give me a good bed of heather, especially when the ripe blooms are pushing their fragrance into my face, the sun is bright and there is something like Reeth to fill the eye.

But we had to move on and really it was not much of a penance because there is always something to see on that unfenced track which climbs between grass and heather, over bridges and streams towards Leyburn.

*(Opposite) Watersplash and Langthwaite, seen regularly on TV in the opening shots of* All Creatures Great and Small. *(Below) Great Punchard Gill*

On the airy summit we saw a single wind-bent tree, symbolising the harshness of the life up there, but on that sunny morning the moorland was smiling and as we passed the many beckside stretches of velvet turf – inviting picnic spots – my mind went back to the happy hours I had spent with my family in these places over the years.

Within a few miles we were over the top and when the familiar bulk of Penhill began to rise on our right we knew we had almost completed the magic triangle.

I always have a feeling of loss at leaving Swaledale behind but it had been a wonderful Pennine walk and we laughed together over the events of the weekend as the road dropped through Bellerby Camp.

Then quite suddenly we were on the outskirts of Leyburn and I realised I was back again in the town which had seen the beginning and end of so many of my Dales memories.

# The Buttertubs and Hardraw Force

One of the thrills of the Pennines is the traversing of the summits from one dale to another. There are many roads and passes where you can do this but I feel that the finest of them all is the Buttertubs Pass between Wensleydale and Swaledale.

This is one of the highest mountain passes in England, reaching a height of 1682 feet, and I remember vividly the first time I crossed it. I was told that it took its name from certain holes in the ground near the top which were called Buttertubs because of their shape.

It was really to see these holes that I undertook the walk but I soon found there were other rewards. The wild hill scenery which unfolds is truly inspiring. I started from the Swaledale side just below Thwaite and turned right between the stone walls on to a steeply rising road, once an ancient foot track, then a cart road, and as I puffed my way upwards I stopped repeatedly to look back at the panorama of the head of Swaledale.

On my left, beyond the wall, the fields sloped sharply away towards a deep gorge but I had covered another mile and a half before I could see the bottom of the gorge with a beck running in its depths.

The road hugged a precipitous drop now and as I climbed, the floor of the gorge climbed with me, a grand sight with the beck coming nearer with every step.

Near the summit I came upon several shallow depressions in the moorland turf. In my ignorance I took these to be the Buttertubs and formed the immediate opinion that a lot of fuss had been made about nothing. It wasn't long before I changed my mind because very soon afterwards I found the real things and they pulled me up very sharply indeed.

I was breathless when I saw the menacing pits, one of them nearly a hundred feet deep, sunk into the flat surface near the crest of the pass. I could not believe that the beautifully fluted rock faces descending into those frightening depths had not been carved out by the hand of man but in fact they were the work of nature – rainwater eating away at the limestone over the centuries to produce this uncanny effect.

What a wonderful part of Yorkshire this is. The view back towards Swaledale is quite magnificent with the gorge shallowing out by the roadside to show the little moorland rivulets which are the beginning of its beck. Cliff Beck it is called and it runs away down into Muker Beck and so to the Swale.

*(Opposite) That solitary tree. The Buttertubs*

There is so much to see up here. I strolled around the long stretches of grass, looking over at the two massive hills nearby, Great Shunnor Fell, 2351 feet, on one side, and Lovely Seat on the other. These names are from the Norse *Sjonar* – a look-out hill, and in the case of Lovely Seat (sometimes locally called Lunasit) perhaps derived from *luin* which means an alarm. Possibly it was used in the old days to send warnings to the settlers in Thwaite in the event of imminent danger.

Many years later I climbed to the top of Shunnor Fell with son, Jimmy, daughter Rosie and her school friend, Tessie Calvert – a lovely name for the daughter of a Yorkshire farmer – and it was something to remember. We started at Great Sleddale and after

*Looking back to Swaledale from the Buttertubs Pass*

savouring the incredible view from the top we dropped down the other side to the Garsdale Youth Hostel where we spent the night.

On that first day at the Buttertubs I could hardly pull myself away but when I did I found that there were more delights in store. The descent on the other side into Wensleydale provided probably the finest prospect anywhere of the hills at the head of this gracious valley and beyond. The enormous grass clad mounds pushed upwards into the afternoon haze – an exhilarating and, to me, reassuring sight. There is something about nature's changeless forms which help to put my own troubles into perspective.

At the bottom of the pass I found I was only half a mile from the famous Hardraw Force. Even during my short spell in Yorkshire I had heard of this 100 foot waterfall. The temptation was too strong and I turned east.

I had to go through a little pub – the Green Dragon – to gain access to a long ravine with a cliff at the far end. I passed what looked like the remains of a bandstand and indeed I learned later that that was just what it was. It had all happened a long time ago, but apparently the acoustic properties of the ravine encouraged some people to start a band contest there. In the late nineteenth century, this became an annual event and famous bands came from all quarters to compete and crowds flocked in their thousands to hear them.

But that was just a dead memory on that day when I walked alone over the grass towards the cliff at the far end. Since 1975 these contests have been resumed on a smaller scale.

The rocks overhang the summit and the falls drop sheer in a single narrow torrent into the dark waters below. Possibly I am over-imaginative but I found Hardraw Scar and its waterfall an eerie place. There was something creepy about that curve of beetling rock; a feeling of oppression. In fact, if I had seen some kind of hobgoblin dangling his legs over the top slabs and leering down at me I don't think I would have been surprised.

It is an impressive waterfall without a doubt and I found that I could walk right underneath it against the rock face and stand there, quite dry, looking out through the falling stream. But I still had that funny feeling . . .

*Hardraw Force*

# Semerwater and Birkdale Tarn

I came to know Raydale and Semerwater very well during my work for Frank Bingham when I often visited the farms around the lake. There is nothing very spectacular or dramatic about Semerwater – it is no Loch Lomond or Windermere – but it is a delightful surprise to come upon it in that land where lakes are few. I know it is very pleasant on summer days to emerge sweating from a stifling calf house and see that long cool stretch of water lapping against the green hillsides.

Normally it covers about a hundred acres but can flood to twice that size. It can change its appearance

*The river Bain flowing out of Semerwater*

remarkably and I have seen it on a day of torrential rain with a howling gale when it lost its placid look and was like a little inland sea with small white-crested waves dashing themselves angrily upon the green banks and inundating the trunks of the trees. Even the hardy hill sheep were crouched in long rows behind the walls, sheltering unashamedly.

It is a grand circular walk, climbing up from Bainbridge with the lake showing in brief glimpses on the way to Countersett, then you can go right round Semerwater and back through Stalling Busk to Bainbridge. It is best done, no doubt, when the sun is shining and one can rest frequently on the grass and look down at the unruffled blue and think of the legend which is part of it.

The old story says that a city lies beneath that quiet surface. One day a poor man with supernatural powers came to this city which was an opulent place.

He tried in vain to find food or shelter among the rich houses and only the poorest tenant took him in. Later he stood by this man's cottage, high on the hillside, raised his hand and cursed the city in these lines.

> Semerwater rise, Semerwater sink,
> And swallow all the town save this little house,
> Where they gave me food and drink.

Immediately a great flood of water engulfed the city and it was seen no more.

One wonders how these legends arise but there is no doubt there is often a thread of fact behind them. One Sunday – I can remember it was the twelfth of December in the early fifties – I did that walk around the lake with son Jimmy and a friend. It was a day of iron frost and to keep warm we had to go at a breakneck pace with our boots clattering and slithering over the frozen ground and thickly iced puddles.

The lake beneath us was a leaden grey sheet with a strangely portentous look. Every time I caught sight of it, the tales about it crowded into my mind. Of course, there had never been a great city in that valley but there were other more rational theories.

Some old local people declared they had seen things beneath the waters, learned authors propounded the possibility of prehistoric dwellings, perhaps on piles which had sunk beneath the mud. The idea of an ancient village being submerged was not impossible and as the dusk gathered fast and I looked again at the inscrutable surface of Semerwater, the thought kept recurring. Maybe there *was* something down there.

Another of the rare stretches of water in the area is Birkdale Tarn and my family and I came upon it by accident one spring day when we had ventured up the hill beyond Keld on the Kirby Stephen road. At the top we parked our car in a little inlet and got out to have a picnic above one of the grandest vistas in Yorkshire.

Sandwiches taste so much better when you can look

*Semerwater and (above) Birkdale Tarn*

out on a sight like that as you eat them. The land drops away steeply from the roadside away down to Great Sleddale, the wandering beck and the huge bulk of Great Shunnor Fell, while away to our right rose High Seat and other great grassy peaks.

After lunch we left the car and climbed the few feet on to the moor top. That was when we stumbled on Birkdale Tarn, a half-mile expanse of water lying flush with the tufted grass of the flat table land.

There is something inexpressibly lonely about this little-known lake in its desolate surroundings but on that particular day its austerity was softened by the innumerable gulls' nests along the rush-lined shores. There were scores of these nests, many with eggs and the birds sitting on them, quite unafraid.

My children were deeply intrigued by the sight of all those hundreds of birds' eggs lying there untouched and safe on the bare wasteland. But that was a long time ago and maybe such things are not so sacrosanct now.

# Richmond

I have often said that I think Swaledale is the most beautiful part of England and it is pure coincidence, I suppose, that Richmond, the town at its foot, appeals to me as just about the most romantic and charming town in the country.

It does not need the glorious river and fells higher up the Dale, it is wonderful in its own right with its cobbled market place, its towering castle, the church with shops built into its walls – a feature unique in all England.

Often when working for Frank Bingham I passed through Richmond and looked with wonder at this ancient church, built around 1150. It has an amazing history. It was allowed to fall into ruin in the mid-fourteenth century and later was used to shelter victims of the great plague of the late sixteenth century. In its time it has been a school, a warehouse, a town hall and a court. It was registered as a church in 1745 and it was then that its shops were built into it. It is now the regimental museum of the Green Howards.

When I first drove through the town, I caught glimpses of cobbled wynds twisting their way upwards among the houses. There seems to be an endless network of these little alleys and streets running in all directions. Narrow, wide, flat and steep. I can remember my little terrier, Hector, to whom *All Things Wise and Wonderful* is dedicated, trotting down one of these alleys when he was the tiniest of puppies. So tiny, in fact, that an old gentleman who passed looked at him unbelievingly and murmured, "Ridiculous, quite ridiculous."

The Norman castle overhanging the Swale is a treasure trove of the past and its superb situation with the river curling round its cliff has been captured in many thousands of paintings and photographs.

It seems almost unfair that a town with the magic of Richmond should be set on the brink of the wild beauty of Swaledale. It is almost an embarrassment

*The ancient town of Richmond*

*An old street lamp, the church with shops built into its walls and (right) the castle on the cliffs overhanging the Swale*

of riches. The story I like best is told by a veterinary friend of mine about a Richmond man who died and went to heaven. St Peter, at the gate, asked him where he was from.

"From Richmond," the man replied.

St Peter shook his head sadly. "Ah well," he murmured, "I'm afraid you aren't going to like it very much up here."

*A Richmond wynd and one of its roads to the river*

# West Witton Bank

The local people refer to a traverse of this road as "going over Stopes", but to me, that ride down Grassgill and Capple Bank will always live in my memory as the time when I had to run my brakeless car into a wall to avoid a flock of sheep which were filling the road.

Readers of *It Shouldn't Happen to a Vet* will remember how I sat for a long time looking down at old Mr Robinson's farm – so near, but with that hill between; and the car in which I sat had no brakes. I could take my life in my hands and go straight down or take a safe detour of several miles. As I wrestled with myself there on the flanks of Penhill, the whole breadth of Wensleydale lay beneath me – Bolton Castle, the winding River Ure and the green face of the fells flowing over towards Swaledale, but I couldn't appreciate any of it at that moment.

In those days, I became adept at putting my little old car into first gear when I descended the innumerable hill roads of the Dales, and it was surprising the speed one attained when relying solely on the gears; but that hill with its horrific bends was something on its own. I finally uttered a prayer and launched myself over the side. Without brakes I literally hurtled down and it is still a mystery to me why I didn't turn over.

Even now when I negotiate those hairpin bends in my modern car with powerful engine and perfect brakes, I marvel at the courage or perhaps foolhardiness of my youth. Not for a thousand pounds would I do the same thing now.

I sometimes wonder if I would have rocketed right into West Witton village itself if it hadn't been for those sheep on the road. . . .

*One of the hairpin bends above West Witton*

# Coverdale

I have said a lot about my deep feelings for Swaledale and Wensleydale and yet it is in Coverdale that I have spent my holidays.

To be exact, in the tiny village of West Scrafton. The word Scrafton, means the "town by the hollow" and the village is a closely packed group of ancient houses around the smallest green I have ever seen.

We stayed in Grange Cottage, rented from the then owner Dr Ralph Dubberley. It is a characterful old house with the green on one side and a deep gill and beck on the other. It was originally one of the granges of the monks of Coverham Abbey and has a magnificent fifteenth-century window stretching from the kitchen into the main bedroom, giving an unusually ecclesiastical look to both rooms. It also means that every word spoken in the kitchen can be heard upstairs.

When we first went there, we had never seen the place and since it was October we were prepared to rough it in a no-frills rural dwelling with its full share of dampness and draughts. We were understandably enthralled when we found a gracious country home, with the central heating going full blast and a pile of logs roaring and spluttering in an enormous fireplace and throwing its warmth into a sitting-room with comfortable furniture.

It was a cold day with frost in the air and it all seemed too good to be true. We thawed out by the fine dog grate, then explored the well-equipped kitchen, the dining-room and the three bedrooms and bathroom upstairs. It was perfect.

*Our holiday house in West Scrafton. (Right) Horse-house with Carlton Moor in the background*

And what did we do in October in West Scrafton? Well, you have only to walk out of the door and look up at the long rocky comb on the crest of Roova Crag to feel you have found somewhere exciting. The Crag overhangs the village from a height of over fifteen hundred feet and it is the pleasantest of strolls to follow the track to the summit, then along to the old mine workings and come back to the village via the beck with its hidden pools and falls which are seen only by the farmers and shepherds. It was fine that October, but foggy on the low country and I spent many afternoons up on the Crag with my dogs, either wandering over the mounds and tussocks or stretched out on the crisp grass, looking at the grey blanket rolling over the plain.

Down there it would be dank and dark but on the Crag it was a glittering world of sun and blue skies with the peace and silence wrapping me round as I lay.

Or there was another, even gentler walk, very suitable when my daughter visited us with our grandchild, Emma. The road up and over the hill to Swineside was ideal for pushing the little girl in her buggy and though it was a short way the feeling of Pennine beauty was deeply satisfying.

On one side, above the stone walls, rose the Crag, leading in a noble ridge over Great Haw, Carle Fell and Little Whernside and on the other the land dipped to the floor of the dale with the steep slopes rising to Penhill and Carlton Moor. The long village of Carlton was like a grey thread against the green.

Swineside itself was remarkable; a huddle of dark stone houses in a hollow of the moor, a lost little hamlet on the road to nowhere, yet, incredibly, from this isolation sprang Adam Loftus who rose to the exalted position of Lord Chancellor of England and whose son was the first Viscount Loftus of Ely.

If I didn't have Emma and her buggy with me, I was able to carry on past Swineside and over a long

*(Top, left) Roova Crag, (top, right) Swineside and (bottom) West Scrafton Moor seen from Swineside*

series of reed-sprinkled fields to Horsehouse village – a fine walk. The way led through narrow openings in the walls, made by placing two long slabs of stone upright among their horizontal neighbours to leave a space through which I could only just squeeze. Clearly the builders of the walls, all those years ago, took it for granted that there were not and never would be any fat men in the Dales.

Coverdale is, in a sense, a hidden place. It doesn't open up at its foot and beckon you in as do Swaledale and Wensleydale. You have to seek it out. Among the softness and gentle green banks of Middleham Low Moor, you would not suspect that just round the corner a secluded valley led between steep bare hills for twelve miles into some of the bleakest country in England. It is beautiful but it is a stark beauty of treeless heights and squat grey houses except at its foot around Coverham Bridge and the Abbey ruins where the amiable surroundings are a delight.

And what else, you may think, did we do on a holiday in West Scrafton? Well, Helen and Rosie did a lot of shopping. Shopping? In those remote parts? Of course. Since we were catering for ourselves, we had to buy provisions regularly and the food shops were abundant and excellent.

*The country near Horsehouse village*

Even in lonely Carlton there was an excellent store and when I saw their selection I thought of the days when I was in my twenties and felt lucky to be able to buy a digestive biscuit and a slice of Wensleydale cheese to sustain me on my rounds. Middleham, too, is splendidly supplied while Leyburn is a positive revelation. That windswept little town on the hillside can fix you up with everything you want from groceries, home-baked pastries and butcher meat to wearing apparel for both sexes. To our surprise, we all rigged ourselves out for the following season with clothes of the highest quality.

Of course, I myself spent most of the time roaming among the fells with an Ordnance Survey map tucked in my anorak. It may not sound very exciting to follow those lines of dots which cross the contours of the hillsides but in Coverdale I found it a continual thrill. Especially when my peregrinations took me to the wild country at the dale head.

I recall one autumn day among that awesome vastness when I had the wonderful feeling of being on the roof of England. Gazing at the enormous grass-clad bulk of Great Whernside, I looked over to where the whole landscape falls away to Wharfedale and at the flanks of the great fell where countless

*The wild, lonely country at the dale head*

centuries had carved out the gullies where unseen streams played and secret waterfalls splashed among their rocks.

And as always, the walls, climbing here higher than ever to undreamed of heights till they disappeared over the summits.

All around, the sweet smell of the miles of moorland grass and the silence, complete except for the distant bleating of a sheep. And the sensation, which is comforting at times, of being quite alone; there was no living creature in sight – just me and my dogs.

*Little Whernside and its deep river beds*

The river Cover has its beginning up here and on that October afternoon I could see it coiling its way with little flashes of silver towards the softer country below, bubbling under hump-backed bridges, between towering slopes with the patches of dead bracken almost scarlet against the yellowed grass.

Standing up there, it was a strange thought that for hundreds of years the main coach road from London to Richmond ran through this desolate country. Dodsley's road book of 1756 stated the distance from London to Middleham as 251 miles and 6 furlongs, and Speight describes the fifteen miles between Kettlewell and Middleham through the pass of Coverdale as one of the most rugged of coaching trips – "a boneshaker" in his own words. He also writes that "No traveller of circumstance would ever have thought of undertaking this journey without previously having arranged his worldly affairs."

He does not exaggerate, because the mind reels at the idea of a coach struggling up the old earthen roads of those days over the precipitous Park Rash from Wharfedale and down the similarly steep and tortuous track into Coverdale.

*The river Cover and one of the gills which feed it*

I followed the route now because the light was fading. Down the narrow road through Woodale, Bradley and Horsehouse, called thus because the pack horses were fed and rested there. On and on towards the dale foot, thinking the while how those early travellers must have looked askance from their rocking vehicles at the barren ramparts of grass and rock on either side.

When I reached West Scrafton, it was late dusk and banks of dark cloud were crowding over the rim of Roova's crest into the last pale light in the sky. But the yellow gleam in the window of Grange Cottage gave promise of an evening of warmth and cheer around that wonderful log fire.

Like so many parts of Yorkshire which have changed little over the centuries, history always seemed nearby in Coverdale. First the Anglo Saxons settled here, then the Danes, and when the Normans swept over the area in a vengeful flood, local tales and the mounds of the dead bear witness to the bloody battles which they fought with the hardy inhabitants before they took up their main abode at Middleham.

The Dale's name is said by Speight to come from the Anglo Saxon *cofa-dal*, because of the caverns

*Bradley (right) and Great Whernside glimpsed from an old shooting lodge*

higher up the valley, but I prefer another theory of *cover*, Ancient British for a stream running through a deep ravine; it is more like the place I know.

In our walks we found many Norse names: Bradley – a broad clearing; Caldbergh – cold hill, and in this high-perched village was born the famous Dr Miles Coverdale, Bishop of Exeter, whose translation of the bible was the first printed in English in 1535.

Beyond Caldbergh, two roads join at Coverham. One goes to Middleham and the other passes the fascinating seventeenth-century manor house, Braithwaite Hall, on its way to the village of East Witton, peaceful and attractive under its hill.

But of course, the jewel of the whole dale is Middleham itself. This town is to Coverdale what Richmond is to Swaledale. I have rhapsodised about Richmond because I think it is unequalled for its beauty and its romantic setting, but when it comes to sheer historical associations I think Middleham perhaps is the winner.

Nowadays its soul is in the many famous racing stables around it and the stable lads with their hands thrust into their breeches pockets as they come in for a pint of beer would laugh if I said Middleham was a glamorous place, but it is to me.

The town is not just rich in history, it is saturated in it. In the beginning there was just the castle and it was known as the Windsor of the North. The castle was begun by Robert Fitzrandolph in 1170 and was connected for many years with the powerful Neville family, one of whom was the great Earl of Warwick of the Wars of the Roses. It is almost incredible that this quiet corner of the Pennines witnessed scenes of princely magnificence, lordly occasions of state, revelries, gorgeous retinues. Also, a long list of

*Two views of Middleham and (far right) the gallops above the town*

distinguished personages came and went regularly. The Nevilles were the Lords of Middleham and Warwick the Kingmaker was the last of the feudal barons.

He lived in regal state in his great fortress, entertaining the greatest in the land. It is said that six oxen were eaten at breakfast and his feasts were sumptuous and lavish.

King Richard III, who married Warwick's daughter, the Lady Anne Neville, lived for a time at Middleham castle and it is believed that his son, Edward, Prince of Wales, was born in the round tower. After the fall of Richard at Bosworth, the reign of the Plantagenets ended and so did the great days of Middleham.

Richard's successor, Henry Tudor, clearly had no great reverence for the castle of his enemy and it was allowed to fall into ruin. In 1646 the castle was ordered to be rendered untenable. Part of the walls were blown away and from then on the ruins became literally a free quarry of valuable dressed stone.

Half of the town of Middleham was built from this pillaged stone and yet, mercifully, the castle remains as one of the most majestic and romantic ruins in the country.

Over the years my family and I have explored its shattered battlements, gazing at the roofless chambers where royal banquets were held, looking sadly at the crumbling walls and the deserted rooms where all the panoply of a medieval court once rolled across the scene.

The splendour is gone and now birds nest among the old stones, but the glamour of Middleham remains, trapped within those stout walls which the predators have left standing.

There remain the keep, the banqueting hall, the site of the deep moat, fed by natural springs till about 1830 when it was filled in, and the chapel.

Another sadness, but perhaps a satisfaction for those who rejoice in the passing of great personal power, is that almost every sign of the magnificent and powerful house of Neville has gone from the town.

So there is much to say about Coverdale which is not apparent on the surface and I suppose most people would conclude that its greatest wonder is the long story of the medieval eminence of Middleham, the blazing pageantry and pomp which once echoed among the grey stones and cobbles of the quiet town. But to me Coverdale is wonderful because of its austere beauty.

When I think of it, I think of Coverhead and the wild country at the head of the Dale, of the aloof majesty of the Whernsides, the empty rolling miles of browns and greens and yellows with the bog pools like dark mirrors under their fringes of reeds.

*Middleham castle ruins*

When the TV crew were filming some of the episodes for *All Creatures Great and Small* near Horsehouse, I was speaking with Ted Rhodes the script editor. He had spent much of his time in the south and the TV series had taken him for the first time through the length of Wensleydale and Swaledale. He had been captivated, but here, in Coverdale, he seemed almost awed.

He looked around him, then turned towards me. "You know," he said, "this is the best place of the lot."

Maybe he was right.

*The wild upper reaches of Coverdale*

# The Lead Mines

In my books I have spoken of the green tracks which wander everywhere over the flanks of the Pennines. They are inviting, they seem to beg for people to walk over them and this is one of the most rewarding experiences I know.

They are soft on the feet of men and the paws of dogs and they lead the walker through airy, delightful country. The strange thing is that they often come to an end at lead mines. Disused mines, of course, but when I first saw them I felt a sense of shock and surprise because when I first came to Yorkshire I had no idea that these beautiful Pennine valleys – Swaledale in particular – were once one of the world centres of lead mining.

I could hardly believe that this green land of silence and solitude was at one time the home of a bustling prosperous mining community.

I was fascinated to learn that in the twelfth century, Swaledale lead roofed French abbeys and the King's castle at Windsor. Many cathedrals in Rome have lead from these remote Yorkshire fells on their roofs.

*A green track at Grinton and the Old Gang Mines*

I find something poignant in the fact that here in this grassy country of dairy cattle and sheep a great industry was born, flourished and died, leaving only the silent relics.

It is uncertain just when the lead mining began, but it is known that the Romans were involved in it. A miner once came across a pig of lead with "Adrian 117–138" stamped on it. But many believe that the mining went back as far as the bronze age. When the later miners of recent history came across signs of their predecessors, they used to say that "t'owd man" had been there before them – a typical terse Yorkshire description of the vast and varied people who had delved in the dark underground tunnels just as they had done themselves.

The ore was carried to smelting mills and then on pack horses to Richmond, Barnard Castle and the Roman camp at Bainbridge.

I used to wonder what caused the deep grooves in the hillsides till I learned that they were "hushes", produced by damming a stream in order to uncover veins of lead. This was the ancient way, but later, shafts and levels were used.

When the industry was at its height, Swaledale and Arkengarthdale between them produced 5,000–6,000 tons of lead annually.

Why, then, did the whole thing decline and disappear? It was because of competition from the continent and other parts of the world. In Spain, the ore was abundant and easily worked and also contained a larger proportion of silver.

The depression hit the industry around 1830 when many families moved to Durham to work in the collieries. Others went to the textile mills of Lancashire. By 1865 it was all over.

As I went round my daily veterinary work, revelling in the crystal air of the high Dales, I used to come upon the dark openings of shafts and levels, black and menacing against the green, and I thought how different my life up here was from that of the bygone men who had to leave the sunshine and the wheeling curlews and spend their days 400 feet down in the dank gloom. It was sad to read the names on the village gravestones of miners who had died in their forties from lead poisoning, chest diseases and rheumatism.

*"Hushes" in Gunnerside Gill and a level in the Sir Francis Mine*

These men had an arduous existence. They sometimes had to walk six or seven miles to their place of work and their wages were very small. They lived mainly on porridge and brown bread – white being a great luxury – and tales are told of how they filed down into the darkness of the shaft with the last man closing the door behind him. Occasionally they lost their footing and plunged to their deaths, one of them, it is said, because he had not knocked the snow from his clogs.

The brutal harshness of their lives seemed almost unbearable to me and my instinctive feeling is that they must have suffered great unhappiness. And yet . . . and yet . . . it is said that old people who could remember the last of the ancient miners declared that the gangs of men often sang as they trudged over the fells to their labours. Apparently they found a kind of glamour in their work, like the gold miners always hoping to hit another rich vein. Also, they prided themselves on their knowledge of the underground workings and on their ability to find their way for miles through the labyrinth of tunnels they knew so well.

To me, there has always been a wonder and a romance about the old lead-mining days and my son Jimmy feels the same way, reading books on the subject and tramping miles over the velvet tracks to see the mines. Possibly our favourite has always been the Old Gang Mine near Gunnerside Gill, one of the oldest and most productive in the country. But I saw to it that when Jimmy was a small boy he kept away from the deadly levels and the shafts which could be 400 feet deep with crumbling edges. They are dangerous places.

*Grinton Smelt Mill and (right) another view of the Old Gang Mines surrounded still by the debris of its productive past*

I suppose it is a blessing in many ways that the mines are closed, but there is sadness too, because for centuries they were part of the lives of a fine and hardy people. Everywhere, tucked away in the valleys, there are the memories – the mine buildings and smelting mills, the heaps of tippings, the "hush" grooves in the hillsides, and the old ruins look desolate among the green glory of the surrounding hills.

But not all the miners left after the depression. Many stayed and in Swaledale became smallholders and sheep-farmers with a few cows. They bred the tough little horned Swaledale sheep who can live in the bleak uplands where others would die. They are like their owners, the dalesmen, spare, durable and eminently to be respected.

To this day, in the peace and serenity of the Dales, it is hard to imagine that the lead mines ever existed. The industry now is agriculture, mainly dairy and sheep farming, which seems so natural to the quiet countryside. But the remnants of those old days have always had the power to lift the hearts of my family and myself. They fill us with sympathy and admiration for the old miners and gratitude for the grass-covered tracks they have left behind them.

*The ruins of Blakethwaite Smelt Mill*

# Snowbound Roads

I hope I don't bring back the old winters just by saying that, except for this hard and snowy winter of 1979, it is many years since we spent months under a blanket of snow; but the fact remains that young people look at me strangely when I talk of the Arctic conditions we used to accept as normal every year.

Sometimes the snow started in November, occasionally it waited till December, but in 1947 – the worst year in my experience – it didn't get into its stride till the end of January.

But when it came down, it kept coming. A real lap-up as the farmers used to say. It obliterated everything and changed our lives for a long long time. The snow ploughs used to follow and take the top off, then the cars flattened the remainder down because salt was not used on the roads at that time. After that came the frost which transformed the surface into a sheet of glass over which we drove at fifteen miles an hour, never daring to apply our brakes on the level places and just tobogganing helplessly down the steep gradients, all the time hoping for the best.

In between there were frequent blizzards and the whole process was started again. To a young Glas-

*Kisdon Hill and a familiar winter motoring scene*

wegian like myself, it was almost unbelievable. Yorkshire, I decided, was the snowiest place I had ever known.

When the wind blew it carved the piled snow into drifts of exquisite beauty and in fact the whole district was transformed into a white fairyland, but I fear the country vets took a sour view of it all.

It meant, by and large, that instead of driving to our cases we walked – certainly over the last few hundred yards of farm road, because as quickly as the farmers dug their roads out, the snow filled them up again.

The tough old farmers of those days were wholly unimpressed by the fury of the elements. Mr Clayton in my book *It Shouldn't Happen to a Vet* reacted in

*A snow plough at work near Gunnerside. Muker (below)*

typically airy fashion when I said I was doubtful if I would be able to reach his farm to treat a beast with a cold. "Road? Road's right enough, you'll have no trouble." The road in question was blocked solidly from wall to wall and I could easily have lost my life in the screaming blizzard which overtook me en route, but Mr Clayton's only concession to the weather was that it was a "plain day".

A shovel was the most important item in our equipment then and I would not have dreamed of leaving the house without one. We were digging our wheels out every day but that didn't always provide the complete answer. You could slip back so easily when you restarted the engine. In Swaledale there is a steep little road from near Grinton to Fremington where I spent an entire afternoon digging, tense with anxiety at the thought of the waiting farmer. Every time I started up I slid again and by nightfall I found I had succeeded in digging out the whole road from top to bottom. At the time I wondered why they hadn't mentioned this sort of thing at the veterinary college.

The snow was so ample and it arrived so regularly that we actually got a ski-lift going on one of the local hillsides. I used to try to finish my work before dark so that I could spend an exhilarating hour speeding down the slopes.

I began to fancy myself so much on skis that in that terrible winter of 1947, when helicopters were dropping bread to the marooned farms in the high country, I travelled on skis to many of these places with a rucksack containing my veterinary equipment. When I was successful and was able to help an ailing sheep or cow, I have to admit I felt rather dashing. The dedicated young vet swooping over the white wastes to succour his patients. It was all right as long as it didn't start to snow again, but several times I was caught in a blizzard on those wide moors and I didn't feel so dashing then. I felt very alone and frightened when I realised I had no idea where I was or in what direction

I was going. After one especially nerve-racking expedition I gave up the idea.

But as I say, those winters with the snow up to the tops of the telegraph poles didn't seem to hold any

*The frozen river Swale*

terrors for the farmers. I can think of Mr Stokill who figured in *Vets Might Fly*. He was over seventy, a smallholder who did all his own work and who put me to shame as he stood in the path of a knife-like blast whistling over miles of snow and getting colder all the time. He wasn't warmly clad – a light khaki smock over a waistcoat and collarless shirt – while I, twenty-four years old and muffled to the eyes in greatcoat and scarf, shivered and gasped.

As he forked the manure, a cigarette dangling from his lips and sending sparks into the wind, he saw me hopping around and thumping my gloved hands together.

He looked around him carelessly as if noticing the cold for the first time. "Aye, blows a bit thin this mornin', lad," was all he said about the weather.

Those old Yorkshire farmers were a hardier type than city-bred me. Mr Stokill taught me a few things that day but by far the best was how to get up a snowy hillside without effort.

One of my patients was in a typical Pennine barn perched so high as to be almost indistinguishable on a fellside three feet deep in snow.

I almost laughed when he said that we were going up there. I told him it was quite impossible, but he ignored my protestations and saddled up a little cob.

"Get a haud o' the tail, lad" he murmured, and mounted up.

I did as I was told and in no time at all was whisked to the top. That was certainly the way to do it.

They say weather comes in cycles and the soft winters of the last twenty or thirty years may have lulled us into a sense of false security. Even the hard and snowy winter of 1979 didn't compare with those long months of howling blizzards in 1947. If they do return, I am quite sure my farmer clients will look out of their bedroom windows at the storm and say the same as Mr Clayton.

"Aye, it's a plain day."

*Drifts in Swaledale. A bleak time for the animals*

# The Village Institute

This old building, boarded up and unused, has a lost look, but it is absolutely typical of the places where Helen and I used to go dancing.

And it was to one of these institutes that Tristan and I took Connie and Brenda on that calamitous night when we all over-indulged and Helen came in unexpectedly and saw me at my least attractive.

A lot of these institutes have been pulled down and replaced by brick structures, but when I first came to Yorkshire they were nearly all of wood, serving little village communities which were probably more tightly knit than they are now.

Looking at the old building in the picture, I can recall vividly the scene behind the timber walls. The floor packed with girls in flowered dresses and young men in their best suits but usually still wearing heavy boots. At one end of the room, a platform with the band – sometimes just a piano and violin or accordion, but on special occasions, saxophone, trumpet, drums and evening dress.

At the other end, tables were laid on trestles and a group of middle-aged ladies dispensed ham and brawn sandwiches, mugs of milk, home-made pies, trifles with farm cream thick on them.

It is sad that many of the institutes have become neglected and forgotten because when I pass this one at night on the way to a call, I often fancy I can hear faint echoes of old sounds – the laughter, the stamping of feet, the tunes of the thirties. *Body and Soul, Deep Purple, Stardust . . .*

*The Village institute, now sadly boarded up*

# Thirsk and Sowerby

Thirsk, I would say, is a happy town. It has a cheerful aspect with its cobbled square and its fretted line of roofs set off by the long ridge of the Hambletons. It has an abundance of good shops with smiling people behind the counters and some splendid inns with welcoming landlords.

There is usually a bustling atmosphere, especially on a Monday market day and there is nothing at first glance to suggest its ancient fame.

Tresche, Tresch, Treussig, Thrysk, Uisge – there seems no end to the different names the town has been called in its history. Etymologists get quite excited about the town and we are assured that it is exceptional and that there is no other place name like it in England. I must admit that I thought it had a Scottish sound when I first heard it.

Anyway, it appears in the *Domesday Book* as "Tresche", vulgarly pronounced Thrusk, and even that is a variation of its Celtic name, *tre-ussig*, meaning the place by the water. Apparently Thirsk began in Celtic times as a scattering of clay and wattle huts along the east bank of its own little river, the Codbeck. *Coed* is Ancient British for wood and there is little doubt that the winding stream where my children

*Thirsk market place with its lovely old cobbles and on a busy market day*

paddled and fished for minnows once made its way through wooded country.

We also learn from the *Domesday Book* that Orm and Tor held two manors there with eight carucates and twelve carucates of land respectively. A carucate was as much land as could be tilled with one plough and eight oxen in a year.

The town is regarded as being the centre of the Vale of Mowbray and lies between two important medieval highways; to the east, the road from York to Yarm, and to the west, the road from Topcliffe to Northallerton and beyond, to Scotland.

Soon after the Norman Conquest, the Lordship of Thirsk and much of the land around it was conferred upon Robert de Mowbray and around the end of the eleventh century the Mowbrays built a great castle on what is now known as Castle Garth. The construction of the castle brought an influx of craftsmen and merchants who settled in and around the site and there the original market developed and grew over the centuries into the busy array of stalls seen every Monday.

Sadly, no vestige of the castle remains today. The Mowbrays revolted against King Henry II and when they were defeated the king ordered that Thirsk castle should be destroyed. The fact that no single relic has been found suggests that the great building was of wood and that it was reduced to ashes.

People walk their dogs over Castle Garth and children play in the hollows of the deep moat but there is nothing else to remind us that a feudal fortress with all its pomp and military splendour once stood on that very spot.

But the pleasant modern town of Thirsk is still very much alive. The cobbled market place is particularly attractive, though the venerable stones are often hidden by the parked cars of visitors. Those cobbles were in danger a few years ago and there was a move to replace them with concrete or tarmac. Thank

heaven, reason prevailed and, though they had to be moved because they had become irregular and pitted with dangerous holes, they were lifted up and reset in a firm base, thus preserving the charm of the town for another few hundred years.

Looking out on the square are many of the shops and inns I mentioned. The two most famous inns are the Three Tuns and the Golden Fleece. The Three Tuns was originally built as a dower house for the family of Bell and is an eighteenth-century building with a very fine staircase rising from the centre of the

*Two old "yards" in Thirsk*

hall. The Lordship of Thirsk came into the Bell family in 1723 and Major Peter Bell is the present Squire.

The Golden Fleece is early eighteenth century and in the old days was the most notable coaching house between York and Darlington.

One of the most charming parts of Thirsk is the Holms, a willow walk by the waterside looking over to Norby, the most northern settlement of the town. I have seen many changes in the Holms. Picturesque old Norby with its mellow brick and narrow alleyways

has been replaced by a modern council estate, and many of the old willows have gone, but possibly the biggest change to me is that the mill which could be reached from the Holms is now dismantled. There is no wheel turning in the water, no great stones grinding the corn.

Helen used to work at the mill as secretary in the early days of our marriage and when I drove down Millgate I was often able to catch sight of her as she bent over her desk. In my memory, she is always wearing a red sweater!

The town is divided into New Thirsk on the west side of the Codbeck and Old Thirsk on the east.

St James's Green is in the old part and some of the houses are of a great age. It has its name from the fact that a chapel dedicated to St James once stood there. Though early records prove its existence, no sign of it remains now. It must have been demolished many hundreds of years ago. Human bones have been dug up, suggesting the existence of a churchyard, and two paved causeways have been uncovered which may have led to the chapel. The Green, as it is always called, is dear to me because it contains the little house which was once Sunnyside Nursing Home and where both my children were born.

In 1768 somebody thought it would be a good idea to increase the town's trade by making the Codbeck a navigable river from Thirsk to the Swale. A wharf was made, and a lock at Sowerby. The scheme was abandoned, but Tristan and I in our daft young days were fascinated by these relics and, as was our wont at that time, composed many fantasies about Thirsk as a mighty maritime port.

Thirsk runs into Sowerby so that the two are often regarded as one but Sowerby is now a separate parish and indeed it has a beauty and character of its own. It has a glorious avenue of lime trees bordering its green, it has fine interesting houses and it has the Flatts. The Flatts are to Thirsk and Sowerby what the Stray is to Harrogate; a spacious sweep of grass preserved as an open place where people can walk with

their children or their dogs, safe from traffic, free to rove widely over the green acres or follow the beaten path by the river's edge.

I have lost count of the times I have walked there, with my children when young, and with several generations of dogs. I know it in all its seasons, when the ground is iron hard with frost, deep in snow, or a shimmering yellow sea of buttercups with the May blossom heavy on the trees, filling the air with its scent.

As you walk, you have a fine prospect of Thirsk with the square tower of the church thrusting above the roofs. To the west there is Sowerby and to the east the hillsides and cliffs of the Hambletons.

The Codbeck flows through the Flatts and it is pleasant to walk along its banks, watching the fish darting in the shallows, catching glimpses of the hills through the screen of trees, moving from the sunlight into the shadows cast by giant willows, gnarled with age, whose branches hang low over the dark water.

My Jack Russell terrier, Hector – to whom, along with my Labrador, Dan, I have dedicated one of my books – lost his sight when he was five. From then until his death at the age of fourteen he ran happily along the criss-cross of paths on the Flatts, confident in his knowledge of the terrain.

There is just Dan and me now, walking the familiar ground as we have done day after day, year after year. At my age I cannot lay claim to athletic prowess but the thought often occurs to me – am I the champion Flatts walker of the district?

I suppose a lady whose house overlooks those gentle fields put it best of all. She met me as I was opening the little gate at the entrance as I had done for several decades and she smiled as she glanced along the track which led over the grass to the bridge.

"You'll know the way by now," she said.

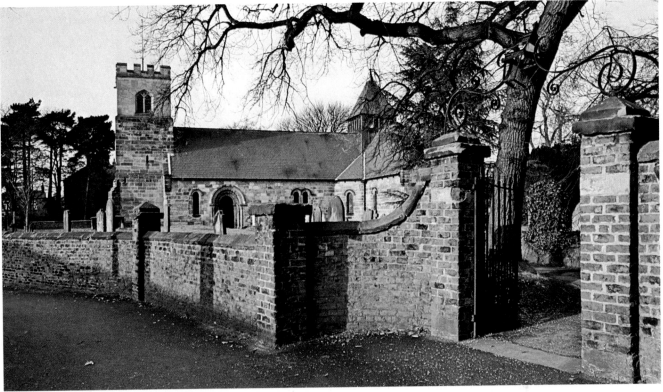

*The Flatts and Sowerby church*

But there are other charms about Sowerby. There is St Oswald's church, originally dating from the twelfth century but almost entirely rebuilt and restored. The Norman style has been preserved in the restoration and the south entrance has a fine Norman doorway, a part of the original structure.

At the south end of the village, there is an ancient pack-horse bridge over the Codbeck. It is quaintly and touchingly known as World's End Bridge and certainly the buildings come to an end there and there is nothing beyond but the green farmland.

In a field a little further up the stream is Pudding Pie Hill, so called because it does look like an apple dumpling or something of the sort jutting abruptly from the surrounding grass.

It is only seventeen feet high but it is much loved by the children of Thirsk and Sowerby and has always been surrounded by legend. In the snow, it made the perfect sleigh ride for toddlers with their first sledge and in summertime when Jimmy and Rosie were just starting to walk, they regarded the seventeen-foot ascent as an Everest-like conquest. It was such a nice shape to climb and you could sit down together on the flat top and look around with the feeling of achievement at the stream, the village, the hills in the distance.

Pudding Pie Hill was reputed to be a fairy house and many generations of children used to run nine times round the hill, stick a knife in the top and put their ear to it in the hope of hearing the chatter of the fairy folk below.

For myself, I thought it looked like a tumulus and when I started to do a bit of research I found that I was right. It was excavated in 1855 at the command of Lady Frankland Russell, and sixteen feet below the

*Sowerby village and World's End Bridge over the river Codbeck*

surface the skeleton of an unusually large warrior was found. His legs and arms were crossed and he had evidently been buried with sword in hand and buckler on breast, though only the handle of the sword and remnants of the shield remain.

Two more skeletons were found, also many bones and pieces of pottery, the jaws of a boar, antlers of a deer, the tooth of a horse, cow's horns and bones of other animals.

It seemed that Pudding Pie Hill had been the burial mound of a small band of the first Anglian settlers in the district early in the sixth century. The warrior chief was there and his friends who had followed him across the sea.

History seems to be always near at hand in this quiet village. Part of the Roman road, Saxty Way, runs near here and we learn from the *Domesday Book* that our old friend Orm of Thirsk had two carucates of land in Sowerby.

It is the same all around the district. Every day on my way to Frank Bingham's practice in Leyburn, I passed an inn on a crossroads three miles outside Thirsk. It was called Busby Stoop. The landlord, thirty odd years ago, was a Mr Ingham and I often used to drop in for a glass of beer with him on the road home. It was over an ale that he told me the grisly story of the origin of his hostel's name.

At Kirby Wiske, at a farm called Danotty Hall where I have calved many a cow, there lived in the seventeenth century one Daniel Auty who was an expert coiner and became very rich at his trade. A man called Busby courted his daughter, married her and became a partner in the business. One night a quarrel over money flared up and Busby murdered Auty. He was tried, convicted and executed and his body was hung in chains on the gibbet at my familiar crossroads. Hence – Busby Stoop.

And just along the road another peaceful village, Topcliffe, hides a glamorous past as it stands high and serene above the Swale. It was for centuries a famous seat of the powerful family of the Percies and a resting place of the kings of England. For eight hundred years the Percies, probably the greatest uncrowned family in Europe, held lands and a manor house here, and quiet little Topcliffe was then the scene of joustings, pageants and tournaments. There are associations in Topcliffe right to the beginning of our history, with the Ancient British and Druidism.

There is abundant interest in the surrounding villages, but when I think of Thirsk and Sowerby my mind goes back to the *Domesday Book* and to Orm and Tor who caught my imagination from the start. What were they like, these farmers of a thousand years ago? Just where were their carucates of land, what animals did they graze on them and who treated the beasts when they were sick? But maybe they didn't bother much with vets in those days.

*The peaceful village of Topcliffe*

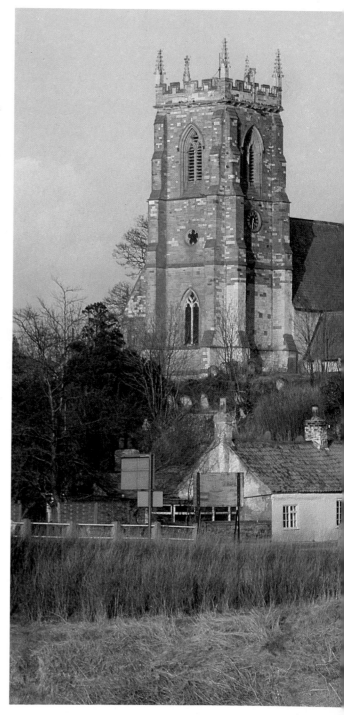

# Thirsk Church

This is the lovely old doorway through which Helen and I walked on our wedding morning.

When I first saw Thirsk Church, it seemed to me like a little cathedral in its style and grace. It is dedicated to St Mary Magdalene, though some say to the Virgin Mary, and must be one of the most beautiful of parish churches with its fine perpendicular architecture and its eighty-feet high battlemented tower dominating the entire town.

It has done this for more than five hundred years and during these centuries the first thing any visitor to the town saw would be that great square tower rising high above the nearby houses.

It is the same today and when I am on my rounds and look down from the hills on that familiar sight I always think of the bitter November morning when Helen and I walked out into the frosty sunshine.

It was Canon Young who married us and I can remember the old gentleman shivering with cold. I think he was glad when it was over and so was I, but as we went outside and the winter sunshine flooded down on us I couldn't help hoping that the old proverb was true. Happy the bride . . .

*The cathedral-like church of Thirsk*

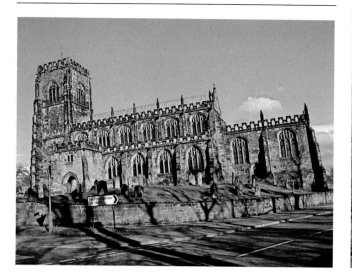

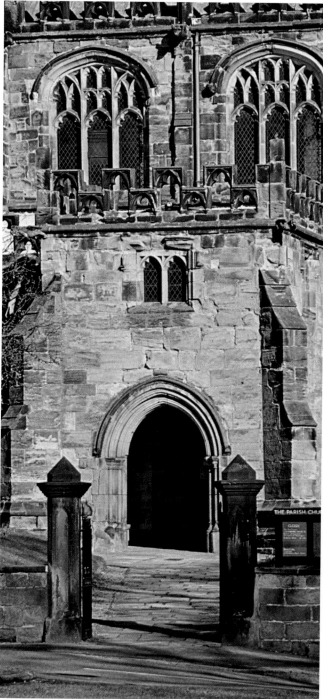

# Honeymoon

People nowadays find it hard to believe that Helen and I had a working honeymoon. We spent it tuberculin testing, partly because the work was overdue and partly because we hadn't the money to do anything very exotic.

For all that, we had a wonderful time. I did the testing and Helen did the writing as I injected the cows and called out their skin measurements. Our headquarters was the old Wheatsheaf Inn at Carperby.

After our marriage on a cold, sunny November day in Thirsk Church we drove west to Richmond. It was in the era when everybody's idea of a big night was going to the cinema, and that was what we did. We went to the Zetland in Richmond, then drove through the darkness, over the moors, down the steep bank to Redmire and so to Carperby.

We hadn't expected anything to eat at that hour but the owner, Mrs Kilburn and her niece, Gladys, produced a delicious hot meal. Those two good ladies fed us like royalty during our stay there, piling the dining-table with Yorkshire fare. Enormous breakfasts of home-cured ham and fresh eggs, massive dinners of roast beef and Yorkshire puddings and apple pies drowned in cream. And always, on the table,

*The Wheatsheaf, our honeymoon hotel, and Sleddale near Gayle*

a foot-high Wensleydale cheese – the old kind of "wet" Wensleydale cheese which perhaps did not satisfy the technical purists but was exquisite to eat.

Our bedroom, with its brass bedstead, looked out over the old roofs of the village houses across the Ure to the hills beyond, and I still feel that wherever Helen and I might have spent our honeymoon we could not have found greater beauty.

This feeling persisted over the next few days when the sun shone determinedly and we drove from one grey-stone farmhouse to the other, luxuriating in the surroundings of Wensleydale and Coverdale.

*Gayle and the bridge over Duerley Beck which runs through it. Typical barns near Gayle*

I can remember Mr Butterfield of Melmerby being highly amused at our kind of honeymoon and bursting into half-stifled laughter as we moved from barn to barn on his farm.

I had a lot of fun, too, with Mrs Allen of Gayle, that marvellous village set off incomparably by its beck rushing over the shelving rock. I was having lunch with Mrs Allen on the Tuesday after testing her husband's cattle when she teased me, as she often did, about getting married. When I replied un-emotionally that the ceremony was fixed for the following day she couldn't believe me.

"But you're coming here to do the second injection on Thursday!" she said.

I nodded. "That's right. And I'll be bringing my wife with me."

"But aren't you going on a honeymoon?" Her eyes were wide.

"Of course," I replied airily. "We're coming here."

*Gayle in the distance and the country nearby*

It was a wonderful punch-line and when I left the farm the poor lady was still incredulous. But all her doubts were resolved when I turned up on Thursday with Helen, and she gave my new wife a proper Dales welcome.

The day was idyllic. The Allen farm stretched away over the high moors to Oughtershaw, a piece of bleakest Yorkshire, but smiling in the sunshine through its bare miles of tufted grass. The air had the sharp sweetness which is found only on the topmost Pennines. And that was where Mr Allen first referred to Helen as my "missus". I really knew I was married then.

A lot of the cattle were housed up there in the stone barns which were scattered over the hillsides, but the ones outside were run down and caught on the open fells by the two Allen sons. This is something I have never seen done anywhere else and to this day I look back with awe on the toughness and endurance of those two young dalesmen.

*The wild moors above Oughtershaw : some of Yorkshire's bleakest country. (Below) inquisitive patients*

# Sunnyside Nursing Home

This little yellow door is the one through which I hurried on the night my son was born. As I described in *Vets Might Fly*, I was, of course, playing hookey from Scarborough where I was billeted with the RAF and I hadn't expected to find I was a father when the bus rolled into Thirsk.

The upper room on the left is where Helen was lying with Jimmy in the cot by her side, and Helen always looks back on her stay there with wistfulness and affection. In those days they kept women in bed for fourteen days after they had given birth and Helen declares it was one of the best holidays of her life.

Nurse Bell – Brown in the book – was a wonderful cook as well as an expert with babies, and my wife recalls that in her busy life it was one of the few times she did absolutely nothing for a long period while being served with delicious food at regular intervals.

Of course it happened again when my daughter, Rosie, was born – in the very same room. This was in peacetime, a little more than four years later, and I was directly involved in the dramatic preliminaries which I had missed the first time. We had been to Harrogate on our half-day and Helen had begun to experience funny little pains in the cinema. These increased on the way home in the car and we had a restless few hours of scares and alarms till 6 a.m. when Helen announced that there was no time to be lost – young Rosie was definitely on her way.

Shaking with panic, I whisked her round to the little Nursing Home on the green, and the first person I saw when I burst into the place was Cliff, Nurse Bell's husband, at his breakfast.

I should think that at that moment the most anxious man in the town was confronting the calmest. Cliff was a perpetually smiling, unflappable, supremely amiable man. He was a lorry driver for a local contractor and over the years he had seen a long succession of distraught husbands standing in that kitchen.

*The nursing home. Rosemary and Jimmy*

He grinned up at me from his laden plate as Helen was ushered upstairs. "Now then, Jim, it's a grand mornin'."

It was the ninth of May and the rising sun brought promise of a fine day, but I wasn't in the mood to notice.

"Yes, Cliff . . . yes . . ." I muttered, most of my attention focused on the creaking of the floorboards in the bedroom above.

He speared one of a selection of sausages which lay among mounds of bacon, eggs and tomatoes, and sliced into it. By his side stood an empty porridge bowl, and a pile of cut bread and marmalade awaited his further attention. He was a very large man but I felt he would not suffer from malnutrition before lunch time.

As he chewed he smiled at me again. "Don't worry, lad," he said, "it'll be right."

And it was right – at eleven o'clock that morning. After hours of classical floor pacing and repeated attempts to read the newspaper upside down I rushed to the surgery phone.

It was Dr Addison's familiar big voice. "A sister for Jimmy!" he boomed happily.

It isn't Sunnyside Nursing Home any more. Our little community has lost the much-loved Nurse Bell, and Cliff lives alone behind that yellow door. He was a devoted husband and he misses his wife sorely, but as you would expect, he is still smiling.

# Back Window and Garden

Helen's fluttering dishcloth from that top window was the last thing I saw before starting my daily round. Every morning on my way up the long garden path to the garage I stopped, turned and waved and the dishcloth never failed to wave back. Behind the window lay our kitchen – a bench and a gas ring against the wall, a table, a stool and a chair, all standing on bare boards.

Beyond that, our living-room, almost as primitive, looked out over the tumbled roofs of the little town to the green hills.

We started our married life up there and have never been happier. Sitting at our bench we could see all of the high-walled old garden with its back-cloth of tall elms where the rooks nested in the top branches.

In those days the wistaria covered the entire rear of the house, thrusting its fragrant blooms into the open windows. Thirty years ago, it was cut down to within a few feet of the ground so that the old brick walls could be pointed, but it is now growing back with all the promise of its former glory.

The many fruit trees along the south-facing wall were removed for the same reason but we have grown some wonderful crops of outdoor tomatoes in that sheltered suntrap.

The french window at the foot of the house opens on to the surgery waiting-room, but in the old days of my books that lovely room with the glass-fronted cabinet over the fireplace was where Siegfried, Tristan and I spent so many happy bachelor hours. After the war, Helen and I lived for eight years in Skeldale House and this was our family sitting-room, open on summer days to the sunlit garden.

They were a hard but happy eight years. Siegfried had married and moved a few miles out into the country but this was still the practice headquarters to which the farmers sent their calls on that ever-jangling phone, and we saw the dogs and cats in the long off-shoot on the left. But most of all, it was home for Helen and me – where we had our early struggles and where we raised our children from babyhood.

I have described the start to my day, with the dish-cloth waving from the top window. The end was just as good. On the winter evenings when I had finished – or hoped I had finished – work, I left my car in the garage in the yard and walked the length of the garden with my eyes on the french window at the other end. It was just a glow in the darkness then, an oblong of light at the foot of the tall old house, but I knew that behind those curtains Helen, Jimmy and Rosie were waiting, bed-time stories were to be told round the fireside. And I never failed to experience the same swelling emotion – thankfulness and gratitude.

The garden itself has not changed so very much. Sadly, the magnificent acacia tree which grew from the centre of the lawn blew down one windy night many years ago.

I was sorry about the acacia tree because it had happy associations for me. On the very first day when I walked into Skeldale House to apply for the job as assistant to Mr Siegfried Farnon, I fell asleep against that tree.

I had waited for hours for Siegfried to arrive, with the niggling doubt growing larger all the time as I reflected that Mrs Hall, the housekeeper, had not been told to expect me, had never heard of me, in fact. In those days when jobs in veterinary practice were almost unobtainable, this call for an interview had been like a life-line to a drowning man and now I was faced with the possibility that the whole thing had been some horrible misunderstanding.

It was to stem the rising panic that I walked out

*Skeldale House – a good view of that top window (the one in the middle) and the garden*

through the french window into the garden where the hot sunshine was imprisoned between the high walls with their stone copings. There was all the peace of high summer there contrasting with the turmoil in my mind. As I sank down on the unkept lawn and leaned back against the acacia tree, I knew nothing of Siegfried's forgetfulness and absentmindedness or I wouldn't have worried and dropped into that uneasy slumber.

But thank heaven when I opened my eyes some time later, he was there, looking down at me and obviously not surprised. I was greatly relieved because, apart from anything else, I had fallen immediately in love with the old house – and I liked the look of him, too.

The giant elms which overhung the yard have also gone but it is easy to imagine the din the rooks used to make high above at nesting time.

And though Helen and I no longer live at the old house and Skeldale is simply our practice premises, I still turn back when I walk up the long path and I can still see the dishcloth fluttering from the top window.

# Pig Sty and Yard

My readers of *If Only They Could Talk* will remember how the pigs swept Tristan aside and made their break for liberty. This sty in the corner of the yard was the starting place of the mad gallop across the yard, through the open doors and via the back lane to the market place. In the grand days of Skeldale House when "t'owd doctor" used a carriage and horses to do his rounds, this yard was in immaculate condition.

Old Boardman described in the book the weed-free cobbles, the saddle room with its shining harness, the loose boxes and stables which were meticulously cleaned and swept out each day. I often pictured "t'owd doctor" standing on the front steps of the old house in top hat, frock coat and gloves, giving the hat a tilt as he waited for the coachman to bring his carriage round from the yard. But these are faded glories and the yard is little used now except to keep an occasional horse in one of the boxes.

The memories remain, however. You can still see the foundations of the massive stocks where Siegfried and I used to fasten the cart horses to dress their feet. The trough is there, silent and waterless, and right in the corner by the pig sty is the old brick boiler for cooking the swill. It defied all Tristan's efforts to make it work but it presented no problems to old Boardman who could have it clucking and bubbling contentedly within minutes while a savoury aroma floated from under its lid.

But in my time the yard's greatest day was when those pigs escaped among the crowded stalls of market day. On that same day, Siegfried's mare got away, too, from the box by the sty and finished up eating the wallflowers in the vicar's garden.

Nearly everybody in our little town kept a pig at the bottom of their garden in the old days but I think those in Tristan's care were the only ones who went shopping on market day.

*The old yard and piggery*

# View from Sutton Bank Top

This is the scene which, during forty years of veterinary rounds, I have observed in all its moods. I have said so often in my books that one of my greatest pleasures is to stop for a few minutes between visits and take my dogs for a walk. I must have stopped at this very spot thousands of times because there is no better place for a short stroll – along the green path which winds round the hill's edge with the fresh wind swirling and that incredible panorama beneath.

They say you can see a train start at York and finish at Darlington from up here. I don't know about that. I have never tried to follow one, but I do know that it is an incomparable view-point from which to study the vast plain of York which stretches between the Pennines and the Hambleton Hills.

Just below is Gormire Lake and beyond, the endless chequered miles of the plain; fields and woods and farms covering the flat, fertile zone which rises gradually in the far west to the soaring bulk of the Pennines.

Every day is different up here and often the far hills are dreamlike with distance, but there are other times, on the frosty mornings or after a night's wind, when you can almost reach out and touch the flat top of Penhill, when you can look down Wensleydale and peep into the entrance of Coverdale with the long summit of Great Whernside rearing above its neighbours. On those days the mighty plain seems like a narrow valley between the two ranges of hills.

On foggy days the flat land below can look like an expanse of cotton wool with tufts of trees pushing through it. Beneath that pall the people of the villages and farms are groping in the dark while on Sutton Bank top the sun sparkles in a sky of unclouded blue.

Above Gormire Lake rises the formidable precipice of the Whitestone Cliff. In 1755 many thousands of tons of rock fell away from this part of the escarpment, leaving a sheer white face visible for many miles.

This is sometimes called White Mare Crag because

*The right-hand side view*

of a legend which describes how the devil in the guise of the Abbot of Rievaulx lured a knight, Sir Henry de Scriven, to his death one dark night. In the course of a wild gallop the Abbot led his victim to the edge of the cliff. The unfortunate knight was mounted on a white mare, borrowed from the Abbot, and as he toppled over the edge to the rocks beneath he looked upwards and saw the Abbot swooping above him. The feet in the stirrups were cloven and horns were growing from his head.

This macabre little tale is told in an old poem by the Rev Richard Abbey, but as one walks this tranquil path today the only swooping to be seen is the graceful dipping and rising of the gliders from the Yorkshire Gliding Club which has its headquarters on the other side of the Scarborough road.

When my children were young, we used to play together among the gorse bushes and moorland grass where now stand two car parks and an information centre. It saddens me in a way that they have replaced the sweet green with tarmac and brick, but I can understand, too, that people from Teesside and the industrial west should want to come up here and savour this beauty.

I know I keep saying these things about Yorkshire, but this is the finest view in England.

*The view of Roulston Scar and Hood Hill from Sutton Bank Top*

# The Old Drovers Road

Of all my walks, this is probably the favourite, a magnificent ridge road a thousand feet above the plain, skirting the edge of the Hambleton Hills. We have tramped it so many times from Oldstead by Steeple Cross, Black Hambleton and Slape Stones to Osmotherley.

I discovered it when my children were very young, attracted by the appeal of a wide grassy highway stretching between dry stone walls to the moorland beyond, where it dwindled to a narrow track among the heather. And all along the way we had only to turn our heads to see the glorious spectacle of the plain of York and the Pennines to the west and the sweep of the North York Moors to the east.

At that time we knew nothing of its history. It was just a lovely walk, but over the years we picked up fragments of its ancient story.

The strange formations of the ground we found in the vicinity turned out to be a long barrow and tumuli, pointing to a prehistoric association. The Romans

*The Old Drovers' Road and the fine view from there*

used the road, so they say, the Scots pursued Edward II's army over it till they clashed at Scotch Corner above Oldstead. But to me, as a veterinary surgeon, the most romantic aspect was the thought of the countless thousands of cattle herded along those beautiful miles. They came from Scotland on their way to the markets of the south and I often tried to capture in my imagination the rough images of that lost race of men in charge of them, the drovers.

Even this part we found out for ourselves. It was on a Sunday afternoon and we had climbed up Kepwick Bank, that delectable winding route to the

*Two more views of the road and the sad remains of Limekiln House*

summit of the Hambletons. Turning north we came upon what we thought was the ruins of a farmhouse and Jimmy and Rosie clambered eagerly among the fallen grey stones.

Then, "Look, Dad!" Jimmy cried. "There's a cave here."

I peered down through the stone slabs to the dark depths of a cellar. We had found Limekiln House.

There isn't much left of Limekiln House now. Much less than there was that Sunday afternoon, but I can visualise it as it was in its great days, with the long stretch of moor at its back, the heathery bulk of Black Hambleton to the north and just over the wall across the green road, that vista of the plain.

Limekiln House was once a famous inn used by the

cattle drovers, a refuge and shelter perched high on the moor top. When we first found it, the outlines of the wide paddock where the animals were stabled for the night could clearly be seen, and later, to my delight, I learned at first-hand the history of the inn.

Mr Luke Kendall of Nab Farm, Kepwick was one of my clients and his grandfather had been landlord of the inn. The old man told me of the nights when the rain-soaked drovers came eagerly into the warm haven, ate their fill of home-cured ham and bacon and caroused far into the night. This part of the business was a sore trial to Mr Kendall's grandfather who had to trail repeatedly down the steps into that cellar my children found to keep filling his beer jug.

Mr Kendall recalls one time when his grandfather

lost his patience. It was two o'clock in the morning and the landlord, heavy-eyed and exhausted, looked around him at the roomful of roistering Scots whose thirst showed no sign of being slaked. He came to a sudden decision. He descended yet again to the cellar, filled two large buckets with beer and bore them up the steps. He placed the buckets in the midst of the singing men.

"Right lads," he said. "You can help yourself, I'm off to me bed."

This is just one of my memories of the Drovers' Road, this romantic green highway trodden by the men of prehistory, the Romans, the drovers, and so many times by myself, my family, my dogs. And I often wonder – is there a better walk anywhere?

# Kilburn

Robert Thompson had come to Skeldale House to consult me about his dog. Helen ushered him into our dining-room to wait for me but when I opened the door I found that something was interesting the old man more than his animal.

He was gazing, entranced, at the long sideboard of French fumed oak which had been handed down to us from Helen's mother's family.

He bent and stroked the wood reverently. "Beautiful, beautiful," he murmured, the gentle, white-moustached face illumined by the great passion of his life – oak.

To me, he was primarily a doggy client, but to others he was the famous Robert Thompson, known throughout the world for his genius as a wood carver.

He was born in this little village under the White Horse and as a young man he was working as a wheelwright when the Parish Priest of Kilburn, Father Nevill, asked him to make a cross of oak, a refectory table and some other things he needed in his church work. He was astonished at the talent shown by the young man and advised him to specialise in making oak furniture.

Young Robert took his advice and a legend was born. In looking for a symbol to distinguish his work he thought of the expression, "Poor as a church mouse" and he chose a mouse. That mouse, an integral part of everything he made, brought people of all nations to his door in the quiet Yorkshire village. He used only oak, seasoned for several years, and made everything by hand, using ancient tools like the adze.

Kilburn is famous, too, for another animal, its White Horse. One Thomas Taylor, a native of Kilburn who left for the south, was inspired by the sight of the White Horse of Uffington in Berkshire, and it seemed to him that the face of Roulston Scar above his old village offered an ideal situation for something of the same.

Kilburn's White Horse was cut out there in 1857 by the village schoolmaster and thirty helpers. It is 314 feet long and 228 feet high and is kept white by whitewash and chalk chippings.

A tremendous celebration marked the completion of the work. Two bullocks were roasted and more than a hundred gallons of beer drunk. This revel was well justified. The horse is a wonderful piece of work, a striking landmark visible from many miles across the plain of York.

*Robert Thompson's cottage and piles of maturing oak stacked outside. (Right) the White Horse of Kilburn*

The upkeep of the horse is helped by the proceeds from the annual Kilburn Feast, held in the second week in July. It starts with sports on Saturday and ends on Tuesday with the Lord Mayor's Show, and the spectacle of the Lady Mayoress, a man in woman's clothes, snatching kisses from any ladies he can catch.

I often pass through Kilburn in my daily work and the place holds many memories. When Helen and I were married – around forty years ago now – we were so captivated by the Thompson furniture that we started a "Thompson Box", a kind of piggy bank for that special purpose. We managed only a coffee table and a couple of ashtrays before nature took a hand and the box became our "Baby Box". Jimmy was on his way and we couldn't afford both.

The Cartwrights, grandsons of the great old man, have carried on the business since his death in 1955 and Helen and I are still among the many who flock there to buy the lovely oaken objects which still have the wavy, adzed surface – and the famous mouse.

# Coxwold and Byland Abbey

About two miles from Kilburn – you might say just round the corner – lies Coxwold, a justly renowned village. Its popularity could be explained simply by its appearance, with its fascinating old houses resting on the slope of the hill; it is really a show village, a picture of mellowness and grace with a fine inn, the Fauconberg Arms. But there are other features which have brought it fame.

One of the most beautiful churches in Yorkshire looks down from near the hill top. It is noted for its most unusual octagonal tower. If you walk a hundred yards north you will find, on the opposite side of the road, the ancient Shandy Hall where Laurence Sterne, the famous humorist and wit, lived for seven years while he was vicar of Coxwold.

In his letters, Sterne declares that he was never happier than when he was at Coxwold and indeed one can imagine that his life must have been pleasant in such charming surroundings and in a house which seems to breathe peace and contentment from the old brick of its gabled frontage.

*Coxwold village and (below) Shandy Hall*

He wrote much of *Tristram Shandy, A Sentimental Journey* and *Journal to Eliza* here and yet for thirty years I knew Shandy Hall only as a farmhouse. The tenant, Mr Charles Smedley, was one of our clients and I have lambed ewes and treated sick calves and bullocks in the building in the rear and drunk many cups of tea with Mr and Mrs Smedley in the kitchen.

The old house has been renovated and is now very properly a Laurence Sterne museum. It was opened to the public in 1972 and can be visited every Wednesday in the summer and any other time by appointment. Some small objects from the author's life can be seen there.

I am glad to say, however, that Shandy Hall is still a dwelling house. Mr and Mrs Monkman, the instigators of the project, live there and this is fitting because the old Hall is the kind of warm and gracious place which should be lived in. Mr Smedley has moved to a smaller house in the village but at the age of eighty-eight he still continues to be a working farmer.

Three quarters of a mile south of Coxwold is Newburgh Priory with its placid lake. It was built by the Augustinians in 1145 and during all the years I have lived in Yorkshire I have listened to arguments as to whether the body of Oliver Cromwell lies there.

The Priory was at one time the home of Cromwell's third daughter, Mary, who married the grandson of Lord Fauconberg. When Cromwell's body was dragged from Westminster Abbey to be hanged and beheaded at Tyburn by his old enemies, it lay for more than two days at the Red Lion Inn, Holborn, and it is believed by many that an exchange of corpses took place there and the real body was taken to Newburgh and immured within its walls.

The mystery has never been resolved because none of the Wombwell family who have held the estates since 1825 have undertaken to open the supposed tomb and there is no sign that they ever will.

*Newburgh Priory*

But there is no doubt in the minds of most of the local people. Cromwell lies in there.

Also near Coxwold stand the noble ruins of Byland Abbey, warmly sheltered from the east wind by the hillside above Wass village. The Cistercians who built it originally settled in the village of Old Byland, high on the moors, but only a few ridges west of the village remain to show the foundations of the monastic buildings.

Two reasons are put forward as to why the monks decided to leave Old Byland and build the Abbey we know today. One is that they wanted a more sheltered position and the other is that they couldn't stand the sound of the bells from Rievaulx Abbey in the valley below.

I should think there is a bit of truth in both theories because you can imagine the wind-blown monks on the hill top listening to those bells and comparing their lot unfavourably with that of their brethren cosily esconced at Rievaulx.

In any case they did leave and erected their beautiful building in a more comfortable place. It was at Byland Abbey that Edward II was resting when the Scots fell upon his army at Scotch Corner and routed it at the Battle of Byland. Edward was forced to flee to York.

*The beautiful ruins of Byland Abbey*

# Harrogate

Those of my readers who know me will have little difficulty in identifying the fictitious Brawton with Harrogate.

I had a half-day off every week and when you are a country vet living on the job it is no good spending that leisure time at home. Your clients will undoubtedly come and winkle you out and you can find yourself using up the precious afternoon in calving or lambing. You need a refuge, a hideaway, and mine has been Harrogate for nearly forty years.

I love my work but it is stressful, and the sense of escape as Helen and I roamed the streets of this lovely town was unbelievable. Even now, when I step from my car in Harrogate, I can feel myself relaxing, feel the tensions and the pressures growing less.

Maybe it is something to do with the gentle air of Victorianism which still hangs over Harrogate, because originally the town was a spa where people came from all over the country to "take the waters", wander in the Valley Gardens and listen to the band.

Almost magical powers were attributed to these waters which were drawn from various wells, notably St John's Well and Tewit Well.

Millions of years ago, a geological upheaval resulted in about eighty mineral springs coming to the surface, mainly sulphur and iron. The springs were first recognised in the seventeenth century when they were reputed to cure diseases of the bladder and kidneys, epilepsy, jaundice and intestinal worms. People also bathed in the waters as a remedy for skin complaints.

The spa steadily increased in popularity and reached its peak in the late nineteenth and the early twentieth centuries. Imposing hydros were built, and around forty different kinds of waters were available at the Royal Baths where they treated rheumatism, sciatica, gout etc.

I suppose most of the clientele were wealthy people who had over-indulged. The affluent Victorians were addicted to their kippers, kidneys, steak, bacon and

*The Royal Baths at Harrogate*

egg breakfasts, vast lunches and dinners and frequent snacks between. They washed all this down with an abundance of wine, spirits and beer, so they needed a place like Harrogate to recuperate as on a modern health farm.

Helen and I, wandering among the gracious buildings, have often amused ourselves by picturing the top-hatted, tail-coated gentlemen and the ladies with their long dresses sweeping the paths of the Stray and the Valley Gardens. On sunny afternoons we sometimes sit around the old bandstand, taking in the gentle atmosphere of those Victorian and Edwardian days.

*The pump room (right) and the town's gardens*

The Stray is probably another reason why we find Harrogate relaxing. It used to be known as the Two Hundred Acres and is a stretch of grassy land preserved as a public place when the common lands of the Forest of Knaresborough were enclosed in the eighteenth century. These wide expanses of green are one of the glories of Harrogate and give an airy grace and spaciousness to the whole town.

Another of the joys of our half-day was that we met Jean and Gordon Rae there. Gordon was the vet in Boroughbridge, escaping like me from the mud, the wellington boots and the telephone, and we comforted each other by recounting our triumphs and disasters of the past week.

Our first meeting was strange. Helen and I were having tea in Betty's Café when a powerfully-built man left a neighbouring table and addressed me in a Scottish accent as strong as my own.

"Are you George Donaldson?" he asked.

I looked up in surprise. "No. Why . . .?"

"Well, you look just like George Donaldson. He was at school with me at Strathallan."

"Oh," I said, "The only chap I know from Strathallan school is Gordon Rae of Boroughbridge."

"That's funny," he replied. "That's me."

Of course I had to start explaining that I had heard a lot about him, but it was the beginning of a long friendship.

For thirty years, the four of us met every week in Harrogate. We used to spin out the stolen hours. Lunch at Betty's or Standing's, shopping in the afternoon, tea at Betty's, then the cinema – there used to be four in the town – and finally a late meal at Louis' Restaurant. Nobody took better advantage of a half-day than we did, because we knew – wives as well as husbands – that another week's hard slog lay ahead.

Sadly, Gordon, the mighty laugher, the talented painter and naturalist, is gone from us now, so we are three instead of four, but Jean, Helen and I still go to Harrogate together every week, drawn there irresis-tibly by the clean beauty of the place and its memories.

The town has changed in one way; it is a popular conference town and holiday resort instead of a famous spa. The spa side of Harrogate went into a decline in the early thirties. There were several reasons: the advance in medical science which suggested that all these ailments could be treated much more simply than by drinking the rather disagreeable waters, there was an economic recession in the country, and rich people had altered their diet to within normal bounds. The Spa Rooms were demolished in 1939 and the Pump Room which contained the old sulphur well is now a museum.

The flowers in the town are exquisite throughout the year but for us the best time is early spring when the Stray is carpeted with crocuses. As we drive from Knaresborough, this tapestry of brilliant colour spread beneath the trees welcomes us with its exultant message that winter has gone.

Harrogate means a lot of different things to a lot of different people, but to Helen and me it is still the exhilarating leisure-place, the town on a hill, blown over constantly by the fresh Yorkshire wind – our weekly haven.

*The Stray, carpeted with crocuses*

# York

When you stand on the edge of the Hambleton Hills above Roulston Scar and look southwards over the plain, you can see, thirty miles away, a towering structure rising from the long stretch of flat land. This is the stupendous Minster of York and it dwarfs the city and everything else around it.

Five hundred years ago, people could stand on this same spot and pick out this mighty cathedral of St Peter, the glory of the city of York, but for those in the city itself there was a wooden chapel on the site as early as the seventh century.

In our courting and early married days, York was where we spent most of our half-day holidays from the practice. In fact Helen bought her wedding outfit there and I suppose if we hadn't met Jean and Gordon Rae who lived so near Harrogate in Boroughbridge, York would still be the venue for our weekly pilgrimage to leisure.

Even so, we have happy associations with the place and love to visit it as do people from all over the world.

We have spent many hours wandering along the 700-year-old walls, exploring the ancient treasures of the place or sailing on the river.

*The Minster towering over the city of York with the river Ouse in the foreground*

In Harrogate we always sense the clinging charm of Victorianism but in York the feeling of history goes much further back. There are memories of the Romans, medievalism, Tudor elegance. It was founded in 71 A.D. and became the northern capital of Roman Britain.

Humbert Wolfe sums it up in his poem when he remarks to London: "York was a capital city when you were a nameless stew."

When Helen and I walk those streets and go shopping, it is a fascinating thought that this very

*(This page) three views of the city walls and the Shambles. (Opposite) the Shambles, a medieval lane leading to the Minster and the Tudor-style gabling of St William's College*

area once echoed to the tramp of the Roman legions. Eboracum was its name then, and hundreds of years later, after the Norman Conquest, it was still the second city of England.

Even now its pride is evident as it displays its wonders. The incomparable Minster, the city walls, and the great imposing gates known as "bars". When I first came from Scotland, I was entranced as Helen led me down quaint streets like The Shambles where it seems you could shake hands between the top windows, and when she showed me the Guildhall, St Mary's Abbey ruins, Clifford's Tower, the Merchant Adventurers' Hall, the Castle Museum, and a score of other gems.

For those who delight in things past, York is a paradise.

*The incomparable Minster*

# Rievaulx Abbey

This takes me back to my courting days. After the disastrous night at the Reniston and the only slightly less ill-starred visit to the cinema, Helen suggested that it might be a good idea if we just went for a walk next time.

We did go for a walk – to Rievaulx Abbey. From the village of Scawton we made our way down the long wooded valley which opened out past two farms to where the narrow road wound towards a little hump-backed bridge over the river Rye. There we turned left and followed the road by the tumbling river and I shall never forget the feeling, almost a sense of shock, as we rounded the thickly clustering trees and I had my first sight of the abbey. I don't quite know what I had expected – probably a few scattered stone relics and an occasional standing column. When the magnificent soaring arches of the Rievaulx choir rose from the floor of the hill-girt valley I was struck speechless and I covered the half mile to the great ruin in growing disbelief.

Helen, of course, had seen it many times before, but as we walked along the riverside road I was glad she hadn't described it to me beforehand and that she had left me the delight of this surprise.

Maybe it is because of this association, but Rievaulx remained in my mind as the most beautiful monastic ruin in England. Yorkshire is rich in its abbeys and many would regard Fountains as the queen of them all, but the sheer grace of Rievaulx touches me most deeply. Founded by the Cistercians in 1132 and set in the heart of the moorland, it is a heavenly place.

The choir, with which I fell in love that first day can be seen, excitingly, from Rievaulx Terrace, a half-mile stretch of lawn on the hillside above the valley. Helen and I walked up there in the sunshine, admiring the two classic temples on the green turf, but looking down again and again, almost in awe, at the tremendous building below us.

Then we went down and wandered through the church, over the cropped grass which flows round the base of the arches with the flying buttresses reaching high above. We examined the few flooring tiles which lie there as reminders of the glory which existed those centuries before.

Rievaulx village is a picture in itself with its thatched cottages, dry stone walls and its background of wooded hills, a piece of rugged Yorkshire hugging the side of the medieval splendour.

Before we left, we took a last look at the abbey, tucked so cosily among the enclosing hills, sheltered from the bitter winds which blow from the northern and eastern moors. Those old monks usually knew where to find a place of comfort and beauty to build their settlements and Rievaulx is a perfect example.

Since that day I have been to Rievaulx scores of times – with my children and their young companions and with friends who visit us. There are many parts of Yorkshire which I delight in showing the people who come to see me, and high on the list is Rievaulx Abbey. I display it with pride – as though it were mine.

*Rievaulx and (right) the choir seen from the terrace*

# Lambing Scenes

This is one of my favourite sights – the new-born lambs turned out with their mothers among the beauty of the upland pastures. It is Yorkshire at its best.

The little groups of families represent a triumph of care and sheer hard work. Lambing time is the most hectic period of the vets' and farmers' year. Some of the farmers, like Rob Benson in *Let Sleeping Vets Lie*, do not go to bed for six weeks. A doze in a chair is all they permit themselves. They have brought the ewes through pregnancy toxaemia, mineral deficiencies, prolapses and all the other pre-lambing troubles and they don't intend anything to go wrong now that the culminating moments have arrived. Often they have to help the ewes with difficult presentations and make sure that the new arrivals are suckling properly, because a tiny lamb born into a night of snow and frost will surely die if it has no food in its stomach.

Occasionally they bring the very weakly lambs in to the fireside or as in the case of Mrs Butler who rescued Moses the kitten in *Vet in Harness* they go into the oven for a spell.

As for the vets, the lambing and other sheep work hits them like a great wave, just when they are at their busiest, because spring is the time when other live-stock are at their lowest ebb, cows and beef cattle having been confined indoors through the long winter.

Of course the vets see only the very bad lambing cases, the ones the farmers know they cannot do themselves. Sometimes it can mean as long as an hour's work, and in the thirties, which is the era of my books, the work was often carried out in the open fields in the teeth of the biting Yorkshire wind and rain.

This can still happen, but nowadays the farmers usually bring their bad cases into a shed or barn where the vet can creep thankfully out of that ever present wind and take off his jacket behind a screen of straw bales.

As I say, it is the toughest part of my working year but at the same time, the most rewarding. Delivering these uniquely appealing little creatures is an unfailing joy and the charm of seeing them struggling to their feet while the mother "talks" to them has never grown dim for me.

The lambing season has another delightful significance. It means that the long harsh Yorkshire winter is almost at an end. The noises that come from the lambing pens and sheep folds are remarkably varied. The low-pitched chuckle of the ewe as she licks her new offspring, the angry, possessive baa-ing when they feel there is a threat to their families, and the shrill bawling of the lambs themselves.

It all adds up to the phrase I use in one of my books – "The sound of the sheep, the sound of spring."

*The windy uplands at lambing time*

# Forestry Roads

I have mentioned in my books that instead of taking a "tea break" in the course of my veterinary work, I stop my car at a suitable spot and walk my dogs.

In Yorkshire, the choice is not difficult because there is an unrivalled selection of grassy tracks in the hills where you can walk in springy comfort for a mile or ten miles. The only difficulty arises when that piercing north-east wind which is so common in this part of the world comes whistling over the moors. The farmers call it a "thin wind" or a "lazy wind", because it can't be bothered to turn aside and just goes straight through you.

In any case, it detracts from the comfort of my few minutes' relaxation and that is where the forestry roads come in. They are more properly called "rides" and they have a secret charm. At any time, they are enticing to walk over with their pine scent and the glimpses of mysterious distances among the dark trunks, but they are most rewarding on the bitter days when the wind is like a knife and the most dedicated walker must hesitate before venturing outside.

That is when I have parked my car on the grass verge by the road and hurried with dogs and children into these havens.

Here you can stroll for miles in shelter, feeling only a freshness and a scented breeze while the wind tears at the branches high above. There is so much to see in this cloistered world; the rich, pink-orange carpet of pine needles among the tight-packed trees, the patches of gold where the sunlight is broken into islands of brightness by the curtaining branches, splashes of winter larch making a warm bronze against the changeless dark green of the spruce.

On still days, the silence is complete and comforting. Sometimes you can hear the busy murmur of a little stream, winding its age-old way which it took so many years before these conifers were planted. A forgotten, hidden stream now, but there to be discovered by those who walk the forest roads.

*Forest at the top of Sutton Bank*

# North York Moors

One of the wonders of my own particular piece of Yorkshire is that anybody traversing it starts in the dramatic isolation of the Pennines, descends into a rich, thirty-mile-wide plain where every yard of the fertile soil is carefully farmed and gentle villages abound, then suddenly comes bang up against the escarpment of the Hambleton Hills where a mere nine-hundred-feet-climb over Sutton Bank brings him back to a land of stone walls and moor.

It is startling, this sudden transition from lushness to austerity and it happens in minutes. That short ascent transports the traveller into a different world. On a night call in winter I have stopped my car in heavy rain just below the summit of Sutton Bank and watched the snow falling steadily on the summit above. On another night I was almost frightened out of my wits when a huge antlered stag appeared suddenly in my headlights, leaped across the car bonnet and disappeared into the darkness.

Thousands of times in my veterinary work and on countless days on pleasure, I have driven over this road – the highway to Scarborough and the coast. The happiest occasions, perhaps, were when I sped off with my family on hot summer Sundays to the North Sea beaches or to tramp the innumerable exciting paths which cut through the lonely stretches of heather.

This is the land of the North York Moors, a unique area of wide vistas and deep gills. It was declared a National Park in 1952 and sweeps away eastward from the Hambletons to the rugged cliffs of the coast.

One particularly memorable expedition to this enchanting countryside was when Helen and I went to see them making my very first film, *All Creatures Great and Small*. This was a tremendous novelty for me because I had never had a book filmed nor had either of us ever met an actor, and there were some very famous ones waiting there over the hill.

As always, when we topped the ridge of the bank

*Farndale ; looking up towards Blakey Ridge*

and headed along the Scarborough road, my first impression was of space. Flat rolling miles of moor and cultivated land in a great wide semi-circle. In August and September this airy prospect, even in the far distance, is purple with the heather's bloom and chequered with the gold patches of ripe corn.

From the top of the escarpment the land slopes steadily to the charming market town of Helmsley, tucked within its hollow in the moors. I have happy memories of the castle ruins there, much beloved of my children when very small. They were especially fascinated by the deep moat, now dry, but still a fine grassy hollow to explore. Helmsley is the start of the Cleveland Way Walk, the second longest footpath in the country, ending in Filey.

Helen and I thought we must have a look at Bransdale on our way so after leaving Helmsley we cut through Carlton and spent a while taking in the glory of this, one of the remotest valleys in the North York Moors.

*Helmsley castle and Bransdale*

We drove up then on the Gillamoor road and stopped the car on Rudland Rigg, that dearly familiar track which we had trodden so often with our children. A golden yellow earthen path cleaving its way through the heather up to the old ironstone railway; no place for motor vehicles with its soft clay and jutting slabs of rock, but a walker's paradise.

We left the car and made our way north and upwards to the windy crest where you seem to be able to see the whole world awash in a billowing ocean of heather.

*(This page, below left) two views of Rudland Rigg. (Top right) the old milestones with phonetic spelling and (bottom right) Bransdale. (Opposite page) sheep file across Farndale*

From where we stood, thirty or forty miles of open country rolled to the skyline.

Oh, the feeling of freshness and freedom up there, with the air keen and the wind sharp, but carrying with it, in the season, the scent of heather.

I often feel that the soul of the North York Moors lies in and around Rudland Rigg because the motif of the whole area is distance and heather.

This is a different Yorkshire from the western Pennines but it has its own magic. Again I must say it – the airy distances, flat at first glance, but when you look again you discern the clefts of numberless gills and valleys. There is a tangy bite in the air which is different, too.

From the Rigg you look down on Bransdale on one side and Farndale on the other, and if you search around this region you will come upon some wonderful old milestones and direction posts with the phonetic spellings of the ancient masons carved upon them; "This Kerby Rad", indicating the road to Kirby-moorside. They wrote it as they spoke it.

Walking down to the car was a lot easier and we drove into Hutton-le-Hole, one of the district's prettiest villages but suffering from a plethora of visitors because of its picture postcard attraction.

Then back up to Farndale to look for the film crew. We soon found them in that long, beautiful valley, famous for its blaze of daffodils in the spring and so like a Pennine dale with its walls creeping up to the untamed moorland.

I could see at a glance that they were filming the episode of the Clydesdale horse with pus in its hoof. I had described it in my first book, *If Only They Could Talk*, and as I looked down the hillside at the actors I was snatched back to that first day when I went to Darrowby and met Siegfried.

There below me were Anthony Hopkins and Simon Ward driving up to the farm in a marvellous old car of the thirties. Their clothes, when they alighted, were of that great period, too, and I watched entranced as the farmer led out the horse and Simon Ward lifted the foot and sweated over it as I had done so many years ago.

*Autumn in Farndale*

People have always asked me if I felt a thrill at seeing my past life enacted but, strangely, the thing which gave me the deepest satisfaction was to hear the words I had written spoken by those fine actors. Both of them have magnificent voices and every word came up to me and pierced me in a way I find hard to describe.

The next thing, of course, was to meet these people and I must say I felt very diffident about that. I waited in some apprehension as the scene was shot and then re-shot a dozen times – something which I was to learn was inseparable from film-making. Then the director took Helen and me down the slope and the moment had arrived.

I have always been puzzled by the fact that Simon Ward, who was playing me, told me later that he was absolutely petrified at the prospect of meeting the real me. For a man who had just made a great name for himself playing Winston Churchill it seemed odd. An obscure country vet was surely insignificant by contrast.

However, our mutual fears were soon dissolved and we discovered we had a natural rapport. Tony Hopkins

*Farndale East*

There was one Sunday when I hung on with clenched teeth and bulging eyes as we hurtled up and down the one-in-three as part of the test during a rally. Actually I didn't last much longer as a navigator as Tony became a little tired of my propensity for guiding him into the middle of woods and dead-end farm tracks and wisely sacked me.

There really was once a chimney on top of the bank – it was a great landmark until it was pulled down in 1972 – and it existed because this was one of the centres of the ironstone industry a hundred years ago.

This, like the lead mining of the Pennines, has been long abandoned and there is the same sad desolation in its relics. Helen and I stood above the remains of the huge calcining kilns, and quite near a long beaten track stretched away – the start of the Rosedale Ironstone Railway which carried the ore over the moors to Middlesbrough and Consett. The view from up there is tremendous and we could just see the three gigantic "ping-pong balls" on Fylingdales Moor.

*The remains of the Ironstone Railway (right). The kilns on the bank top and (left) the view from there*

Simon Ward had told me that he and his wife Alexandra were living in Lastingham during the filming and on our way home we veered off to take another peep at that appealing village.

This, like Rosedale Abbey, is full of charm – sheltered and comfortable, yet with the wildness so close at hand. I could understand why the Wards had fallen in love with the place and with Yorkshire in general. In fact, Simon often said to me that he would like to give up acting and be a vet in Yorkshire, and I think he really meant it.

A monastery was built here in 654 A.D. and destroyed by the Danes around 866. In 1078 monks came from Whitby and built another monastery on the same site. Later they made the long journey to the flat terrain of York where they founded St Mary's Abbey.

Lastingham, of course, is most famous for its crypt and Helen and I went past the ancient gravestones into the church and descended the few steps into another age. There is not another crypt like this in Britain and it has remained practically unaltered for nearly a thousand years. To stand among those age-old stones was a moving experience.

That was the end of our day but I can remember so many other days on the North York Moors.

*Three views of Lastingham*

# A Day in the Captain Cook Country

I remember when we first decided to show our children the Captain Cook country. Cook was a Yorkshireman and the places associated with him are scattered within the north-east corner of my part of Yorkshire. The romantic idea of a farm labourer's son from the fringe of the moors who later became a world-famous mariner and navigator has always gripped my imagination. His explorations covered the Pacific from the Antarctic to the Arctic and yet, after starting life as a farm worker himself, his next job was the very prosaic one of apprentice grocer.

Our way took us past the Carthusian Mount Grace Priory lying back against the wooded slopes of the Cleveland Hills, It was founded in 1398 and I knew it well since I had often treated the dogs in the beautiful old house adjacent to it and the cows in the farm nearby.

Then we passed through Stokesley, a gracious place, full of the character which comes from fine old houses of all shapes and eras looking over cobbles towards a pleasant green. We then turned off to Marton where Cook was born in 1728. Marton was then a small village as indeed was Middlesbrough on the banks of the Tees, but the present day town has spread mightily and Marton is one of its suburbs. It is not surprising that the two-roomed thatched cottage where James was born has disappeared.

In 1736 the Cook family moved to Great Ayton and it was around this village that young James spent his boyhood. The farmer for whom his father worked could see that the boy was very bright and helped with his schooling.

We drove to Great Ayton and walked through the village, by the banks of the Leven which flows so gracefully by the roadside. The wide stream rippling between the rows of stone houses gives Great Ayton a special appeal and the four of us enjoyed a quiet stroll by the water. But, like other followers of Cook, we were unable to see the cottage where he lived. In

*Great Ayton and the river Leven*

1934 it was dismantled and taken to Australia where it now stands in the Fitzroy Gardens, Melbourne, and though it is sad that it has gone it has forged a permanent link with the country with which he was so closely associated.

However, we did see the impressive monument to the great man on Easby Moor. It stands sixty feet high and looks away over Kildale and the moorland country which must have been so familiar to him in his childhood.

When we restarted our journey we came almost immediately upon Roseberry Topping, an interesting hill with trees on its lower slopes and a bare pointed summit which makes it look like a little volcano. Jimmy and Rosie have climbed it several times and it is pretty certain that young James Cook spent many hours up there. It is one of those inviting hills which just asks to be climbed.

*Captain Cook's monument. (Above) the view from Easby Moor and (below) Roseberry Topping*

Squire Skottowe, who employed James's father, apparently decided that the young man should cease being a farm worker. No doubt the job did not require the intelligence which it does today. In any case, the good squire concluded that the occupation of grocer and haberdasher was more suitable for his young protégé and he arranged for him to be apprenticed in that trade in the shop of Mr William Sanderson in the fishing village of Staithes. This was a fateful move.

Staithes, then, was our next objective, and a half-hour drive took us to the coast. We made our way through the newer part of the town right down to the Cod and Lobster Inn which looks over the harbour. We turned right and the whole world changed. We were in old Staithes with a row of infinitely varied houses looking down on a small sandy beach with stone breakwaters at the harbour mouth and the whole village hugged in by two arms of crumbling cliffs.

The entire place breathes the very essence of the sea; the gulls screaming over the tiny harbour, the waves driving in from the far blue, and rushing, white-crested, between the breakwaters, the little fishing boats drawn up on the shore, the men in dark jerseys, oilskins and sea boots, the big red door of the lifeboat house.

We walked round to where a ravine cuts its way to the sea on one side of the village, and here the magic was intensified as we stood on the metal bridge which spans the Roxby Beck, running down from the moors. Beneath us were more boats pulled up by the side of the trickle of water and we gazed wonderingly at the old houses hanging from the sides of the ravine – they were like something from a fanciful picture. Staithes was supposed to have been the haunt of smugglers in the past and it struck me that they couldn't have chosen a better spot.

It is easy to understand how young James Cook fell in love with the sea and ships in these surroundings. They used to build ships in Staithes in his day and I

*Fishing boats at Staithes*

can imagine him looking through the window of his grocer's shop as the salt spray dashed against the glass and everything he saw pulling at his adventurous nature.

That shop, in fact, was so far down on the sea front that it was finally washed away, and no trace of it remains today.

Erosion, of course, is the curse of all this coast with its soft clay cliffs, and much of Staithes stood further out to sea than it does now. I spoke to an old fisherman and he told me that the Cod and Lobster Inn had been washed away three times in its history. He said he had witnessed the last time. "Hundreds of bottles o' beer floatin' out to sea," he murmured sadly. "A terrible sight."

In Church Street there is now a little yellowish-white house called "Captain Cook's Cottage" and it bears a plaque erected in 1978 by HRH the Prince of Wales. It says: "This is stage six in the heritage trail of Captain Cook from Marton to Whitby. Here Captain Cook gained his taste for the sea and ships in this harbour village where he worked as a grocer's assistant for Mr William Sanderson for eighteen months up to 1745."

It was hard to leave Staithes. It is an almost uncanny piece of the past bound in by its two headlands. These cliffs are typical of this fine coastline and in fact at Boulby Head, near to Staithes, are the highest sea cliffs in England, rising to 600 feet.

But we had to follow Cook to Whitby, because his grocer days were finished when he was apprenticed to the Walker family who were coal shippers in that town. He did, in fact, make his first trip from Whitby in a collier by the name of *Freelove*, and it is possible that this first experience gave him an admiration for the Whitby colliers. It is a fact that all his memorable voyages were made in vessels of this type.

As we approached Whitby, we came upon the sea village of Sandsend. The long stretch of beach and the charming cluster of houses make this an ideal holiday spot with the emphasis on peace and tranquillity.

*Captain Cook's cottage and (right) Sandsend*

Like so many of these Yorkshire coastal villages it rests beneath a spectacular headland, in this case a grassy cliff whose summit seems to have been gouged out in places by a giant's hand.

We walked along the little row of dwellings, breathed in the salty air and watched the hundreds of seagulls standing to attention at the water's edge. I could understand why Sandsend was for many years one of the favourite holiday places of Tristan, the colourful character of my books. When his children were young, it was an annual pilgrimage for him.

We came in to Whitby by the coast road but I
always think the best way to approach the town is over
the two moorland roads from Pickering and
Guisborough. First, the sea comes into view, next
the abbey on its precipitous cliff and then you almost
tumble out of the heather into the town.

On our Cook expedition we drove first to the West
Cliff, the modern part and surely one of the most
striking seaside towns in England. To see it on a
summer day, lying high and airy, with the sun glittering on the white fronts of the hotels and the sweep of
grass above the miles of golden sand is enough to lift
anybody's spirits.

But this most attractive and picturesque resort is
something James Cook never saw. The Whitby he
knew was the old town on the other side of the Esk.
This river, after winding through its beautiful valley,
cuts right through Whitby to the sea and on the east
side the old houses cover all the lower slopes of the
hill.

As we rounded the corner of the West Cliff we came
suddenly upon the statue of Captain Cook overlooking
this superb view. The rows of smart hotels were
forgotten and we were gazing down on a scene that
could not have been very unlike that which the great
sailor saw when he journeyed up this way.

Those houses climbing towards the twelfth-century
church of St Mary with the dark dots of the gravestones by its side and the renowned 199 steps straggling
up the green. And right on the cliff top, the abbey
ruins. My long held theory that the monks always
chose warm, sheltered spots to build their great
churches was exploded when I first saw Whitby
Abbey, because it would be difficult to find a bleaker
or more exposed place than that cliff top facing out to
the cold north sea.

There would have been one very big difference in
Cook's view and ours, because as we looked down on
the harbour we could see only a few fishing boats

*Whitby harbour from West Cliff*

while he would have seen a great bristle of masts springing from the pack of sailing ships there. Whitby had been a fishing place for centuries but in Cook's time it was one of the most important seaports in England. It was also a ship-building town.

How fitting that this statue should look forever upon the harbour from which he sailed and upon the great wide sea which was his domain. Whenever I stand there the whole story seems almost too romantic to be true: the farm lad from the moor's edge who ranged the oceans of the world, explored and charted great new lands and met his death at the hands of natives in Hawaii.

Only a few weeks ago I returned to the same spot where I had taken my family those years ago. The bronze features still look out over that lovely scene to the sea and I felt the old thrill.

The main plaque on the statue is to commemorate the men who built the Whitby ships, *Endeavour*, *Resolution*, *Adventure* and *Discovery* used by Capt Cook RN FRS, and the men who sailed with him on the greatest voyages of exploration of all time, 1768–71, 1772–75, 1776–78. It was unveiled in the presence of the High Commissioners of Australia and New Zealand on the 26th August, 1968, the bicentenary of his first voyage. Underneath, it says, "To strive, to seek, to find and not to yield."

There are other plaques to commemorate more feats of the famous mariner; his landing in British Columbia, his discovery of the east coast of Australia, his exploration of the Australian east coast and of the islands of New Zealand. Incidentally, a fine new Captain Cook Museum was opened in 1978 in Stewart's Park, Marton, and relics from Cook's life can be seen in Great Ayton, Staithes and Whitby.

Near to the statue is the spectacular Whalebone Arch to remind us that in those old days fifty-five sailing ships from Whitby were engaged in whaling.

*Captain Cook's statue looking out to sea and some of the waterfront houses*

Whales, polar bears and seals were brought back in great numbers, and houses alongside the harbour rendered the blubber into oil. Those whalebones also preserve the memory of Capt Wm Scoresby Senior, inventor of the crow's nest. He was the most successful and daring of Whitby's whalers and once sailed within 510 miles of the North Pole.

But I have to roll back the years to that first day of our exploration of the Cook country when our children were young. It was time to begin the journey home and we decided to complete the circular tour by taking the moor road to Pickering. We were leaving Cook's territory behind us but there were other different things to see. We drove first through the village of Sleights, then up through the heather and bracken on to the moor.

*The whalebone arch (below left) and the view from one of the many alleyways which lead down to the sea. (Opposite) the harbour*

On this road you have the real feel of the extent of this wild and desolate area. To the east the stark landscape runs down to the sea and to the west there must be around thirty miles of it sweeping away to the escarpment of the Hambletons. There are fertile patches, pretty villages and many farms out there but it is all stolen from the moor, from the bracken and heather which grow most naturally on this bare and windswept region.

Of course it is beautiful in itself, particularly when the heather is in bloom, and as I said, it has lovely villages. We turned right to see one of them – Goathland. This is quite fascinating – one of the few settlements which have not dived for cover in some sheltered valley. Instead it has elected to sit up apparently unperturbed on the flat moorland, taking its fill of the sharp clean air. The motif of Goathland is spaciousness. The attractive houses face each other across what most people would call a wide village green, but when I first saw Goathland it struck me that no green existed but that the houses all had broad frontages of grass giving them a special air of elegance. I have never been able to rid myself of this impression.

With its excellent hotels and splendid setting it is not surprising that Goathland is a popular holiday place for country lovers and for walkers in particular. Beck Hole and the waterfall of Mallyan Spout are only two of the attractions nearby.

We cut back to the main road and after driving for a few minutes through country with sheep scattered among the heather and dark beckoning gullies cleaving the rolling miles, we arrived at the Hole of Horcum.

This is an immense and awesome depression in the moorland, and since the road skirts it, we got out of the car and stood on the rim. The children gasped in wonder as they looked down because there is something almost frightening about this sudden drop into a great bracken-lined bowl with some cultivated fields in the far depths. We could make out two farms down there, and I felt it must be strange to live one's life in an enormous amphitheatre. In November, this place is

particularly impressive with the bracken flaring deep red-bronze.

But this was the end of our day. After a last peep downwards and a final gulp of the sweet air we got back into the car and drove the few miles to Pickering and on to home.

*(Below) Wheeldale Beck and a stretch of the Roman road near Goathland, preserved as an ancient monument. (Opposite) Goathland and moorland nearby*

# Holidays on the Coast

My oldest friend, Alex (or Sandy) Taylor from Glasgow was at one time assistant estate agent to the Marquis of Normanby whose home is Mulgrave Castle, near Lythe, and this led to my family and myself spending an unforgettable weekend on the Yorkshire Coast. Lord Normanby had a cottage in Runswick Bay and generously offered the use of it to the Taylors. We were lucky enough to be asked along.

You seem to topple into many of these fishing villages and Runswick Bay is an extreme case. Nowadays there is a steepish road leading down to an ample car park but on that first visit twenty-five years ago, the access to the bay below just seemed to disappear over a cliff top. I was used to driving over hilly roads but I stopped, got out of the car and peered warily over the edge.

It looked an almost sheer drop but Alex with his wife Lynne and little daughter of the same name ventured confidently on to the frightening incline in his Land Rover. I followed very slowly, my family packed into my old Austin A70, my hand thrusting the lever into bottom gear.

One advantage of crawling downwards at less than walking speed was that the beauties beneath were gradually unfolded. The sparkling blue sea, a grand stretch of steep cliff with a fine headland, and a warm and inviting stretch of sand.

When we reached the foot we could see it all. On the right, the long curve of cliff and the beach, and on the left the exquisite little village sprawled on the hillside with a jumble of rocks leading from the lowest house out to the lapping waves.

Small boats of all descriptions were scattered along the sea front and there were plentiful signs of fishing gear. The big red lifeboat house with its slipway down to the sand dominated the beach and I had heard many times of the brave rescues carried out by the lifeboat crews there.

I find it difficult to convey my feelings as we walked

*Our holiday cottage at Runswick Bay*

through the village. The children in particular were captivated by the maze of steps and narrow sloping alleys which curl among the houses. These houses seem almost to sit on top of each other; they are of many colours, white, grey, brown, most of them very old but some newer, and as we threaded our way up, down and across we tried to count the number of ways you could traverse that little pack of dwellings. We never arrived at any definite conclusion.

The cottage right at the bottom, flush with the rocks beneath, was Lord Normanby's and during the two nights we slept there, it was exciting to listen to the waves beating against the stout wall of stone outside.

We had a wonderful weekend there, Jimmy, Rosie

and little Lynne spending much of their time fossil-hunting among the rocks and on the beach. There was an abundance of fossils, especially ammonites.

When the time came to leave, I was sad on two counts. I felt I was leaving behind something wonderful as I looked at the village nestling close to its sheltering cliff, and also I wasn't looking forward to climbing back up that hill which hid Runswick Bay from the ordinary world.

Alex roared up without much trouble in his Land Rover but I decided to let my family walk – they didn't need much persuading because I think we all felt that my car which had done more than 100,000 miles would stand a better chance of reaching the top without them.

However, all was well. I ground my way up slowly but successfully, though I must admit that when the flat land appeared on the summit my jaws were aching through a prolonged clenching of teeth.

But as I said, there is another road now, and the thousands of holiday makers who visit Runswick Bay no longer have any worry in that respect.

I would like to recall another happy time we spent on the Yorkshire coast – with the Taylors again. This was not just a weekend but a proper fortnight's summer holiday and we spent it at Robin Hood's Bay.

It does seem rather a long way from Sherwood Forest but there must be some reason why the village got its name. Certainly a determined and long-standing legend persists that Robin Hood used the village as a refuge when pursued and that he kept several boats in readiness to make his escape out to sea. It was an ideal spot for his purpose because it is well hidden.

Whether the legend is true or not does not matter a great deal because Robin Hood's Bay is a dream place. Like Runswick, it is so picturesque and scenic that it hardly seems real.

*Runswick Bay and a street in Robin Hood's Bay*

It clings to an almost precipitous cliff-side with one long street straggling down the middle from the top to the slipway on to the shore. There is a strand of sandy beach under the cliff, then a long expanse of rock reaching out to the sea with islands of sand here and there.

Naturally, since our children were very young then, we spent most of our time on the beach, but the start of each day was a treat in itself. That journey through the length of the village had a fascination which did not fade.

Holding the little girls' hands, we made our way each morning down the long flight of steps and the steep roadway, peeping from side to side at the little alleyways, some with tiny gardens and doorways facing each other a few feet apart. There is a stream, too, by the side of the road, a bewitching little stream

*Robin Hood's Bay and (right) the precipitous cliffs at Ravenscar*

hidden by a stone wall. Trees grow from its depths and overhanging houses look down on it from high on the other side.

Every time we reached the narrow entrance to the beach at the foot I had the same feeling – of delight at the ancient charm of the place, and amazement at how the masons of long ago had ever managed to build a whole village at that incredible angle.

Rosie and little Lynne were busy for hours among the rock pools. They would have been about three

years old at the time and I can see them now, small stomachs outthrust as they strutted importantly with their buckets again and again from the water to the holes they had dug in the sandy islets.

Alex, Jimmy and I had some favourite walks. One of them was along the beach to Boggle Hole, a pretty tree-lined indentation in the cliffs forming a sandy cove into which the tidal waters flow alongside a Youth Hostel which Jimmy was to visit many years later during his own exploration of Yorkshire.

And there was another, more ambitious walk, also along the beach, to Ravenscar: slithering over the rocky slabs for five miles, then clambering up the cliff-side to the hotel on the top where we often had tea before taking the high path over the cliffs back to Robin Hood's Bay.

Ravenscar is, of course, the end point of the famous Lyke Wake walk, a gruelling forty miles over rough moorland from Osmotherley, and to accomplish it is a very real test of endurance. I am proud of the fact that both Jimmy and Rosie in their later years have done it.

Helen and Lynne took things a bit easier than the rest of us, and who could blame them? The weather was fine and they were very happy sitting on that slim stretch of sand chatting, watching the little girls, and looking around at the sweep of the bay.

Jimmy used to enjoy one game greatly – dodging the waves as they dashed up on the slipway at high tide, but its popularity waned when he mistimed his run one day and was thoroughly soaked from the waist down. I was just learning photography then and I have a very bad picture of the fateful moment. It is streaked with light and indistinct but still manages to capture the anguish on his face.

As in Staithes and most of these coastal villages, pieces of Robin Hood's Bay have been washed away. I hope the sea does not claim any more of it because it holds some warm memories for me. It seems to epitomise the charm of the Yorkshire coast, a wonderful holiday place which still breathes the atmosphere of its fishing past.

# Scarborough

Those towers on the Grand Hotel which dominates Scarborough have special memories for me. I used to sleep up there with the other airmen on fire picket during the war. And it was while doing sentry duty in the big doorway on a cold dark night that I recalled the story of farmer Bailes's dog, Shep, (described in *Vets Might Fly*) and his sense of humour which I felt I needed at that moment.

The square in front of the hotel is where the unfortunate Cromarty made his ill-timed leap and across which I stole when playing hookey to visit Helen.

I was unfortunate in spending the winter months in Scarborough, but doing PT in singlets and shorts in January and February on the wind-swept prom didn't blind me to the beauty of the place. The morning parade at 7 a.m. in the inky blackness did not allow much sight-seeing but as winter lengthened into early spring I became conscious, as I stood stiffly among the blue ranks, of the golden curve of sand stretching away under the cliffs towards Filey and of the great blue expanse of sea dancing and sparkling under the early sunshine.

I made up my mind then to come back after the war and I have done so repeatedly, with Helen and the children on holiday. And in that peaceful time I also fell in love with the other delights of the Yorkshire Coast – Whitby, Staithes, Runswick Bay, Robin Hood's Bay. You can hardly go wrong.

The beaches are fine, the villages retain the character of their fishing history and always, just in the background and often within walking reach, are the glories of the North York Moors where sea and heather mingle magically.

But still, among all the beauty it is the Grand Hotel which has the most memories because of those six months in the war when we slept in the uncarpeted rooms with the windows nailed open, marched around the echoing corridors under the shouts of the Special

*The sands and the Grand Hotel, Scarborough*

Police and clattered up and down the stone service stairs.

After the war I got a tremendous kick out of taking Helen to dine in the elegant room which was once an open terrace where I learned to use an Aldis lamp. It was glass-fronted when we went there in peace time and as we ate we looked down at the lights of the town winking in the gathering dusk. It was very pleasant, too, to sit in the richly carpeted lounge and drink tea

*The hotel and the doorway where I stood guard*

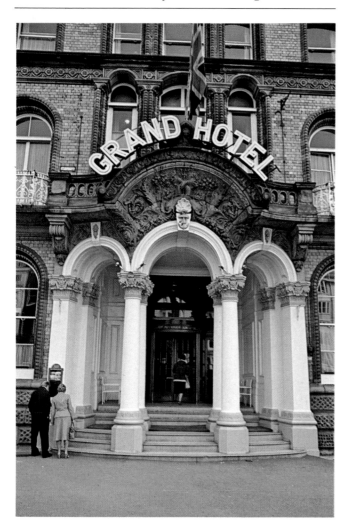

and listen to a string orchestra playing selections from *Rose Marie*, and know with happy certainty that nobody could order me to do anything.

Scarborough is of course divided into two. There is the North and the South Bay, both fine and spacious with splendid beaches. The bays are divided by a headland where the ruins of the twelfth-century castle stand.

I spent a lot of time among those ruins during the war, because that is where they marched us to practice shooting with every imaginable kind of firearm. In fact there are few streets in Scarborough which have not heard the thump of my RAF boots or the slither of my plimsolls. Scarborough is where the RAF converted me from a slightly tubby, pampered, newly-married man into a kind of human greyhound.

They ran us for miles and miles above the Spa in one direction and to Peasholm Park in the other. We trotted up and down Oliver's Mount. We sprinted along the sands and drilled and did PT interminably on the promenade in front of the Futurist Cinema.

The RAF made me fit and it was tough going. But all the time I was aware of many things – the salty, tangy air, the glory of its golden bays, the fascinating mixture of the old and new in the buildings of the town. Fine modern hotels and the old houses of the original fishing village running down to the harbour with its rows of fishing boats and the ever present redolence of the sea.

I could fill pages with our happy times in Scarborough over the years: the Cricket Festival in September when we have been able to sit in the sunshine and watch the great players of history in action while snatches of music from the brass band in the corner drifted over on the breeze. Bradman, Miller, Harvey, Hutton, Compton, May, Trueman, Cowdrey. The list is endless, the memories blissful.

Once Jimmy, Helen and I saw Richie Benaud hit five

sixes in succession off Roy Tattersall and my small son was so overcome that he wanted to go and play *Waltzing Matilda* outside the Australian dressing room on his tin whistle in the hope that the great man might come out and give him his autograph.

I must mention one rather earthy occupation to which Helen and I are addicted and which is somehow symbolic of Scarborough. Working our way along the delectable row of shellfish stalls down by the harbour, selecting little bowls of cockles, mussels, whelks and, when in funds, oysters. Shaking on pepper and vinegar and swallowing the gorgeous things before picking out a crab and some kippers to take home. And all around us the rich, unforgettable mélange of tar and salt and fish and seaweed. Ah, Scarborough . . .

*Scarborough: a wonderful place for relaxing summer holidays*

# Postscript

I have tried to paint a picture of my Yorkshire from the Pennines to the sea, but now that I have finished I feel that I have only flicked at the canvas with my brush. Many knowledgeable people will be aghast at the omission of their favourite haunts and I have suffered in my turn at having to leave out so many villages and hills and streams which have warmed my heart over the years.

However, I find comfort in the thought that these words and pictures may strike a responsive chord in many who love this area and who have trodden the same paths as I have. And especially I hope I have done something for the readers of my previous books who have never seen Yorkshire. In literally thousands of letters from far corners of Britain, from America, Canada, Australia and other distant parts of the world the same phrase has recurred: "I wish I could see the places you write about."

If this book can reach those readers, it will give them at least a glimpse of the countryside where I have found so many of the good things of life.

*Sunset over Coverdale*

# Index

CAPTIONS FOR PRELIMS AND ENDMATTER
TITLE PAGE *Swaledale from Oxnop Common*
DEDICATION PAGE *Bransdale*
CONTENTS PAGE *Bishopdale Beck, Wensleydale*
THIS PAGE *Sheep on the Pennine Way*
OVERLEAF *Outside Reeth*